Strolls & Walks
from
Cotswold Villages

by Gordon Ottewell
& John Roberts

WALKWAYS

****

WALKWAYS
J S Roberts
8 Hillside Close, Bartley Green
Birmingham B32 4LT
****

Strolls & Walks
from
COTSWOLD VILLAGES

by Gordon Ottewell & John Roberts

ISBN 0 947708 29 4

First Published 1994

WALKWAYS

DaywalkS Footpath Networks

Chaddesley Woods
Clent & Lickey Hills
Cannock Chase
Vale of Llangollen
Wyre Forest

The first two are currently in folded A2
sheet format, sold in a plastic cover.

Strolls & Walks

From each of about twenty places there is a
stroll of a mile of so and a walk of 4 to 6 miles.

Strolls & Walks from Picnic Places (Midlands)
Strolls & Walks from Midland Villages

Long Distance Routes

Step by step guides in both directions which
often connect with each other and Long Distance
Footpaths. (A2 sheets folded to A5,
but Heart of England Way is a book.)

Llangollen to Bala   Bala to Snowdon
Birmingham to Ludlow   Ludlow to Rhayader
Rhayader to Aberystwyth
Birmingham to Church Stretton
Heart of England Way

8 Hillside Close, Bartley Green, Birmingham B32 4LT
(Send sae for current list & prices.)

Quercus

... publishing interesting books ...

Quercus publishes books about Wales and the Midlands. We are interested in trees and landscapes, history, battles, lords and kings, castles and churches, meadows and flowers, bridges and tunnels. In fact we are interested in anything that you find interesting.

Currently in print are "Midland Castles", "The Trackway of the Cross", "Sketches of Halesowen" and "Midland Woods & Forests".

Future titles include "Midlands Parks", "Midland Rivers & Streams", "Midland Lakes & Ponds", "Midland Ghosts & Hauntings" and "Australian Williams".

We are always interested in ideas and proposals for new titles If you have an idea but do not think you are up to writing about it, talk to us anyway. We might suggest coauthorship with you providing the research.

8 Hillside Close, Bartley Green, Birmingham
B32 4LT   021 550 3158
(send SAE for further details of books in print)

THE
OPEN SPACES
SOCIETY

Registered charity 214753

The Open Spaces Society

IMAGINE a world without any accessible open space - where land is fenced off, concreted over, built on or otherwise exploited. Impossible?

Commons, greens, city parks, school playing-fields, even cemeteries - any of these could be under threat today. Many would be lost if it were not for the vigilance and expertise of the Open Spaces Society.

These precious places give us room to breathe and a chance to escape from the pressures of life in the 1990s.

If you care about the future of our open spaces, please join us. For membership details write to:

>   The Open Spaces Society (Dept WW)
>   25a Bell Street
>   Henley-on-Thames
>   Oxon   RG9 2BA

We all need open space
for physical recreation
and spiritual refreshment.

(iii)

To enjoy the best of the countryside

Join The Ramblers.

Explore the many hundreds of thousands of miles of Britain's beautiful footpaths and receive our exclusive Yearbook full of information on walking and places to stay.

Plus regular colour magazines and newsletters — free of charge.

You will also be entitled to valuable discounts at outdoor equipment shops.

And at the same time you will be helping us to protect the countryside and to look after Britain's footpaths.

For further information and an application form, drop a line to:
The Ramblers' Association, 1-5 Wandsworth Road, London SW8 2XX

The Authors

GORDON OTTEWELL comes from Derbyshire. He worked ten years as a colliery surveyor before becoming a teacher. Joining the drift south in 1964 as head of a small Cotswold primary school, he has remained in the region ever since.

Now retired, Gordon devotes his time to exploring the Cotswolds and nearby areas and to writing guidebooks and articles. He lectures on rural matters and leads walking groups from as far away as Canada and the United States.

JOHN ROBERTS was born long ago, worked twenty years in insurance and served time as a Loss Adjuster. Then for seventeen years he was a college lecturer teaching law and insurance.

While working as a lecturer he took up walking Midland canals and later footpaths. John became a walks writer and self publisher some ten years ago and is now a full time publisher of the WALKWAYS and QuercuS imprints.

Gordon contributed the local Cotswold expertise, selected the villages. worked out the routes for the walks, did the research and wrote most of the notes. John then walked the routes and wrote the directions. expanded the notes. added some purply descriptive bits about the landscape, took photos and drew the maps. Then they argued about the rest.

Photo Judith Goodman

Upper Slaughter

Contents

The Cotswold Hills & Villages

The Cotswold Hills are a massive limestone ridge stretching one hundred miles between Bath and Chipping Campden. In most places it is about ten miles wide and as a whole, tilts to the east.

The higher western edge slopes sharply to form an escarpment, the northern part falling into the valley of the Warwickshire Avon (Vale of Evesham) and the southern into the Severn Valley (Vale of Gloucester and Vale of Berkeley). Generally the high points lie between 250 and 300 metres; no great height. But these smooth round hills and whale backed ridges are loved for their dramatic and noble contours, steep green slopes and towering views to the north-west over the vast flatness of the Severn Valley.

The structure of the ridge is deeply divided on the south-west edge by the deep, steep valleys of the River Frome and its tributaries, which flow through Stroud.

The eastern side (a dip slope) declines more gradually to the Wiltshire Avon and the Thames and is cut by the valleys of the rivers Windrush, Coln and Churn. But they are not deep or wide enough to be important divisions in the structure.

The massif was formed in the Jurassic period between 100 and 170 million years ago when this part of Britain was submerged beneath a vast, shallow, sub tropical sea. Since then it has been parched, raised, ridged, folded and finally, rasped by ice. The melting of the glaciers some 10,000 years ago was the latest major geological event. Great walls of ice gouged their way from the north, east and west, carrying shattered rock and mineral debris from Wales, Scotland and north-east England. Their grinding action, and later erosion by the flooding meltwater, created the coombs, cliffs, valleys and smooth flanked hills that you see today. Rain drained over the sharp slopes and the limestone rock, some was thrown off and some was absorbed, to give clear fast streams and thousands upon thousands of springs.

The Cotswold ridge is part of the great Jurassic belt which stretches from the Humber to the Dorset coast. The Mendips, Edge Hill, the Northampton hills and Lincolnshire Wolds are part of the same structure. Comparing the pleasant outcrops to the north with the Cotswolds, you may think that we have the best of it.

Cotswold limestone is called oolitic (egg stone) because it is made up of a mass of granules resembling fish roe. Its origins under a warm sea are seen in the numbers of fossils which are the remains of prehistoric sea creatures. Although usually described as honey coloured, it varies considerably over the region and can be any shade from creamy grey to pale buff, silver grey to orangy brown. It is fascinating to travel north-east up the Jurassic belt and compare the textures and tints of the buildings.

Whatever its shade, Cotswold stone has one outstanding quality. When freshly quarried it is soft and easily worked, but when exposed to air it hardens. This combination of convenient features made it famous as a building stone for countless beautiful towns, villages, churches and stately homes.

Gloucestershire claims most of the Cotswolds, though parts reach into Worcestershire, Warwickshire, Oxfordshire, Wiltshire and Avon. The county names and boundaries are modern creations of man, but people have lived in the Cotswolds since at least the New Stone Age. These people where the first settlers in the area some 5,000 years ago and threw up great long barrow tombs which dominate the landscape, such as Belas Knap and Hetty Pegler's Tump.

Neolithic remains in the Cotswolds are remarkable but few. Later Iron Age remains - camps, forts, round barrow tombs are everywhere. The Romans also found the fertile,

Vale of Evesham from above Ilmington

Guiting Power

(4)

well wooded landscape very much to their liking because it could support a large population and produced revenue. Cirencester lies on the site of the Roman town of Corinium, which was second only to London in importance. From this hub spread a network of roads - Fosse Way, Akeman Street, Ermin Street, giving access to all parts of the country. Romans and Romanised Britons built at least twenty villas in the Cotswolds and no doubt more remain to be found. The best known and preserved is at Chedworth and well illustrates the point that the Romans must have spent a lot of time in the bath. Of thirty two identified rooms, one third are connected with bathing.

Chedworth and other Roman structures are now ruins, and it was medieval prosperity based on the wool of the Cotswold Lion sheep that gave the region its superb buildings. Between 1350 and 1500 Cotswold Wool Merchants became some of the wealthiest people in the land, and the great houses, churches, towns and villages that we see today were built in this period.

The Cotswolds have seen good and bad times, but much of their beauty is a product of those distant boom years. Today the region attracts the rich and the retired who modernise labourer's cottages and opt for rural life. With the decline of traditional industries and changes in agriculture, many of the working people and their children no longer live in the villages. So the physical structures of the Cotswolds have been beautifully preserved, it has been described as stuffed, but the social and economic structures totally altered. Tourism has joined agriculture as a staple industry and encouraged fosilisation; any attempt to rock the arcadian boat is strongly resisted. This may appear out of step with the times, but at least it makes for pleasant walking.

Books of walks are intended to give you an experience of places and the landscape rather than mere descriptions. We have tried to give impressions of each village, but we are walkers and hack scriblers, not poets. They have to be seen to be believed. Again, we have sketched in some history, but for detail must refer you to the leaflets and booklets on local features which can be found in most villages.

Many authoritative books have been written on the Cotswolds but we recommend one which is recent, superbly detailed, well illustrated and comprehensive - "The Cotswolds" by Geoffrey N Wright, David & Charles 1991 ISBN 0 7153 9318 9. More specialised but delightfully informative is "Hallowed Ground" by Hilary Lees, Thornhill Press ISBN 0 946328 38 2. Lavishly illustrated with fine photographs and rubbings, it describes Cotswold churchyards, lychgates, gargoyles and most of all, tombs.

From most of the villages we have described a walk of about four or six miles; and because some people are young with short legs, or old with tired ones, there is also a stroll.

The Country Code

* Enjoy the countryside and respect its life and work
* Guard against all risk of fire
* Fasten all gates
* Keep your dogs under close control
* Keep to public paths across farmland
* Use gates and stiles to cross fences, hedges and walls
* Leave livestock, crops and machinery alone
* Take your litter home
* Help to keep water clean
* Protect wildlife, plants and trees
* Take special care on country roads
* Make no unnecessary noise

Boots and Clothes and things

These Strolls and Walks are all modest affairs and you do not need to go equipped for mountaineering. The advice offered below applies to the usual range of Cotswold weather; in the height of summer you might wear almost nothing and we would give totally different advice for extreme winter conditions.

Your best guide to suitable clothing and equipment is your own experience, but if you have none you might like to consider the following points.

(1) Boots. Most people seem to prefer them at most times of year; go for the lightest that you can find. Trainers are excellent in dry weather and very adequate in the Cotswolds.

(2) Socks. You don't necessarily need two pairs, but a good thickness of woolly padding is a great comfort. The traditional grey rough wool "rag sock" is hardwearing and reasonably thick, but that is about all. Try loop pile socks.

(3) Gaiters can keep you comfortable through mud, flood and undergrowth. You can keep them on in all but the hottest weather.

(4) Jeans are cut too close for easy walking. Denim may be fine in California where it was first used by a Mr Levi to make working trousers, but here it is hot in summer, cold in winter, holds the damp and is in any case heavy and stiff. In summer try polycotton trousers, which are light and dry in no time. In colder weather corduroy is not bad.

(5) Take a waterproof, preferably hooded and long enough to reach down to your knees or gaiters.

(6) Take a hat and gloves and something to keep out the wind such as a showerproof jacket. Your waterproof would do, but they can be sweaty and uncomfortable. Always carry an extra sweater.

(7) Think about a long sleeved brushed cotton shirt which opens all down the front. You can wear it open or buttoned to various degrees, or not at all, with sleeves rolled up or down, inside or outside your trousers, and have ventilation or protection from sun, wind, vegetation, insects, as required.

This is general advice based mainly on ordinary clothing. Visit a good outdoor equipment shop and see if they have anything to improve your comfort. There are windproof garments, special hats, and magic vests which do not stay wet like cotton T shirts. First though, try ordinary clothes to find out whether and how they could be improved upon.

Rights of Way & Obstructions

These strolls and Walks are all on public rights of way or well established paths and tracks. They may be Footpaths, Bridleways or Byways (usually green lanes or tracks) with some stretches of ordinary road. Your rights as pedestrian are the same on all, you are entitled to follow the track or cross the land. The fact that it is "private" (most land is) is quite irrelevant.

Occupiers of land are legally obliged not to obstruct paths, it is an offence, but sometimes they do. Paths should not be ploughed up nor have crops growing over them, nor should you meet barbed wire fences. You are entitled to cross or remove any such obstacles doing as little damage as you reasonably can. You may diverge to pass the obstacle so long as you go no further than is necessary and do not enter someone else's land.

These notes are standard to all WALKWAYS books, and it is very unlikely that you will meet any such problems in the Cotswolds. The County Councils take an active interest in rights of way and fund and organise the Cotswold Warden Service. These volunteers are mainly retired people who inspect paths, get obstructions removed, put in stiles and erect signposts. If you meet a Warden, smile nicely and say thank you. If you should be unlucky and meet any difficulty, please write or phone WALKWAYS and we will refer it to the proper quarters.

In the countryside generally the Ramblers Association and other more local footpath groups have an important role in keeping footpaths open. The RA has Footpath Secretaries for each area who monitor the state of paths, respond to closure and diversion proposals and organise maintenance. If you use footpaths it seems right that you should support them. See their advert at the front of the book.

Changes & the Amendment Service

The countryside changes all the time, even in the Cotswolds.
You will sometimes meet new tracks, stiles and barns; hedges
vanish and paths may be diverted. To keep directions as up
to date as possible we issue amendment slips.

IF you write to tell us of any changes or problems
that you meet, stating route and paragraph number,
we will refund your postage.

IF you send a stamped addressed envelope with a
note of what publication(s) you have, we will send
you up to date amendment slips. (Phone enquiries
welcome; 021 550 3158)

Using the Directions

You will see that the Directions are quite separate from
description and comment, very terse and set in short, narrow,
numbered paragraphs in a clear and open typeface. These and
less obvious features have been adopted after much experience
and thought. The aim is to give you information in easily
located and remembered blocks of convenient size, and bearing
in mind that you will be reading them on the move.

Distances in YARDS or MILES are just to give you a rough idea
how far you need to walk. You do not have to try and measure.
Distance in PACES are there to be counted out, if you need
to. Paces vary but you can allow for being very tall or short.
The reason for all this is that people carry a pace with them
but not usually a measuring tape, and very few of us have got
a clue what 200 yards looks like.

Bale tomb at Windrush

Little Barrington's Norman Church

List of Villages, Strolls & Walks

Village	Stroll	Walk	Pge
	(Miles)		
Adlestrop	1.5	6.5	(15)
Ampney St Peter	1.0	4.5	(22)
Bagendon	1.7	3.0	(27)
The Barringtons	2.0	7.0	(32)
Bibury	1.5	5.0	(37)
Bisley	1.5	4.0	(42)
Blockley	1.0	3.5	(47)
Broadway	1.7	6.0&5.0	(51)
Bourton on the Water	2.0	6.0	(58)
Chedworth	1.5	5.0	(65)
Cobberley	2.0	4.5	(71)
Guiting Power	2.3	4.5	(76)
Ilmington	1.5	5.0	(80)
Minchinhampton	1.5	5.0	(86)
North Nibley	1.5	4.0	(90)
Painswick	2.0	5.0	(97)
South Cerney	1.5	5.5	(102)
Stanton	3.0	5.0	(108)
Turkdean	1.5	6.0	(114)
Whittington	1.3	3.0	(118)

The maps are only sketches to a rough scale of
1.5ins/mile. The symbols are obvious. Note
that small arrows mark the start and direction
of Strolls and Walks. Selected paragraph
numbers are shown to confirm your position.

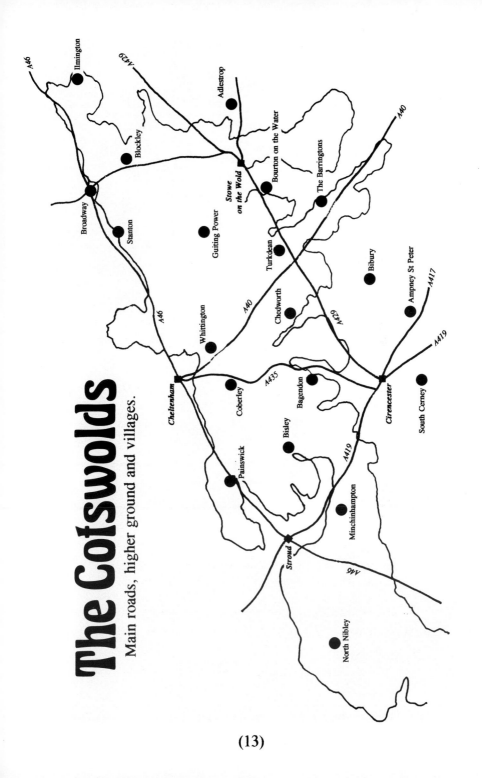

The Cotswolds

Main roads, higher ground and villages.

(13)

Church of St Mary & St Margaret, Adlestrop

Adlestrop

WHERE
Map reference SP 242273, a village off the A436 about three
miles east of Stow on the Wold.

PARK & START
Village Hall car park, and make sure that you leave at least
50p in the donations box.

THE VILLAGE
Adlestrop is a single sleepy street of rich brown and grey
stone houses amongst level fields in the valley of the River
Evenlode. The main street is a loop with a branch to the
church, and when you reach the upper part you find that it
has climbed, giving views over the village. There is a red
brick and thatched Post Office and some unlikely topiary in
the shape of a snail in a village of gardens. But it is more
famous for a poem, perhaps the least important work of the
most important poet of World War I;

> Yes. I remember Adlestrop-
> The name, because one afternoon
> Of heat the express train drew up there
> Unwontedly. It was late June.
>
> The steam hissed. Someone cleared his throat.
> No one left and no one came
> On the bare platform. What I saw
> Was Adlestrop - only the name
>
> And willows, willow-herb, and grass,
> And meadowsweet, and haycocks dry,
> No whit less still and lonely fair
> Than the high cloudlets in the sky

And for that minute a blackbird sang
Close by, and round him, mistier,
Farther and farther, all the birds
Of Oxfordshire and Gloucestershire.

Edward Thomas 1878 - 1917

Soon after his train journey Edward Thomas was killed in
action. He never saw the village and the station has long
gone, but the connection is celebrated in a bus shelter. Here
rests the station name board in nostalgic Great Western
chocolate and cream, and beneath is a railway bench with a
brass plate bearing the poem.

The Rector has published a small anthology of Adlestrop poems
(well - verses then), most of them parodies on Thomas. You
might get a copy from the church or the Post Office.

A more substantial literary connection exists with Jane
Austen who stayed three times at the Rectory (now Adlestrop
House), with Thomas Leigh, her mother's cousin. She was
more distantly related to the Leigh family of Adlestrop Park,
to which there are monuments in the church. There is evidence
that local events and scenery appear in her novel "Mansfield
Park". The great house is Georgian in period (1762) but
gothic in style by Sanderson Miller, an architect who also
designed follies and grottoes.

The small church of St Mary Magdelene was largely rebuilt
in the 18th century. All the windows at the east end are
arresting, the east window itself is a riot of Victorian
colour. A design of formalised flowers in the south wall
contrasts with geometrical designs. The blue painted ceiling
seems to need a few repairs, and you can imagine anxious eyes
straying to it if the sermon ever falls short of enthralling.
Visit in summer to see the churchyard roses.

The Walk visits two other hamlets. Chasleton has a vastly
tall, square windowed and slightly macabre manor house built

in 1603. It seems that the interior and furniture are original but very decayed. It has been acquired by the National Trust who have repairs in hand, and it may open in a couple of years' time.

St Mary's church is simply finished with some low and massive pointed arches on squat Norman columns and a very sturdy plain font. In total contrast is a white marble memorial, high on the wall and proudly untouched by time, garnished, ledged, enscrolled and pedimented. There is another contrast between the fragments of medieval stained glass preserved in one window, next to another showing the polished complexity of Victorian technology. Look for the small, plain-shaped but decoratively carved wooden pulpit. Across the road is a distinctive four gabled dovecote.

The hamlet of Evenlode gives its name to the river which rises nearby. There is a neat green and some handsome farm houses. The Norman church of St Edward is small with the only plain east window we have seen in the Cotswolds. The homely pulpit has funny gargoyles and is some 500 years old.

Jane Austen described herself as a "desperate walker", and like you, she followed the local lanes to visit nearby villages. You should only finish in this condition if it is pretty muddy.

THE STROLL
A level 1.5 miles which is mainly on field paths. You pass a very worthwhile piece of farming conservation, cross a glorious park with a lake and pass a cricket pitch. The lake attracts coots, mallards and waterfowl, while the parkland suits woodpeckers and nuthatches. If he had left his railway carriage Edward Thomas would have liked it.

(1) From car park go R. ✱
Pass house L to drive &
take corner stile L.

(2) Cross field diagonally
& cross bridge.

(3) Go L on field edge
path appx .4 mile to stile
& lane.

[By the brook you can see
young beech and ash
hatching from their
plastic tubes, but most
of the planting is common
alder. On this waterside
tree the short, round
female catkins resemble a
small fir cone which
hangs on the tree all▲

winter. The wood was used
for tool handles and to
make clogs. On our visit
the alders were twittering
with finches.]

(4) Go L, pass lake, &
▲*take stile L just before*
junction.

(5) Go ahead to pass thro
tall trees (R of brown &
white pavilion) & meet
pitch boundary fence.

(6) Go R & around boundary
& take gate to track.
Follow up to church.

(7) Follow lane to T
junction & go L to start.
●

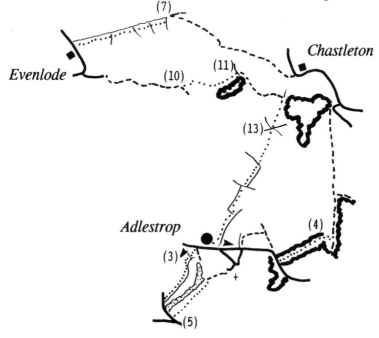

(18)

THE WALK

About 6.5 miles on field paths and green tracks, with a couple of surfaced lanes. On second thoughts, make that brown tracks. This route is not free of mud in damp weather, but it does have a beech avenue with interesting shrubs and a superb hillside walk with stretching views.

✱

(1) From car park go L. Pass lane R & on appx 250yds to take track L.

(2) Follow round R bend & cross field to trees & track. Go R to lane bend.

(3) Go L appx 130yds & take stile L into avenue. Follow appx 600yds to its end, & take stile.◤

[These towering trunks show that beech does well on this alkaline soil. But the varied shrub layer is also interesting, with holly, ash, sycamore, elder, yew, laurel and box. Laurel is easily mistaken for rhododendron. Box only develops a six inch diameter trunk but its hard, heavy wood was used for rulers, mathematical and surgical instruments, kitchen utensils, wood sculpture and printing blocks. It is found only in a few places in the south-east counties and this area.]

◀(4) Go R & round field edge to corner gate. Take track L. At wood end pass track R & follow banked track ahead, to enter trees & take stile to lane.

[By the bench is a little wooden topograph, so you can read off the high points. Is it slightly misaligned? Uphill, the bump is an Iron Age tumulus.]

(5) Take lane L & down appx .6 mile (past lane R, church & big house) to R bend & post box.

(6) Take No Through Road L, round R bend, & on appx ¼ mile, to pass track R & meet gate ahead.

(7) Take small gate L. Go with hedge on your R over 4 fields (.6 mile) to road at Evenlode.

(8) Go L past post & phone box appx 350yds to R bend, & take No Through Road L. ▶

(9) Follow appx .8 mile to end of surfaced lane (which bends R thro gateway).

(10) Take field edge track ahead to pass farm on your R. Go appx .5 mile with brook on your R, & later wood (past inviting gates), to wood corner with steel gates ahead & R.

(11) Take gate R. Follow wood edge track, then green lane, up to gate & field.

(12) Take small gate R & go AHEAD, angling slightly from wood L. When you see it, head for skyline tree & take gate/stile beyond.

(13) Go ahead midfield to projecting hedge corner & take stile. Go with hedge on your L, & via 2 stiles to long field

(14) Go with hedge on your R half way to end, then bear L & take L corner stile. Go with hedge on your L back to start.

St Mary's Churchyard - abandoned in the fields

Ampney St Peter

WHERE
Map reference SP 082014, a village off the A417 Cirencester-
Fairford road

PARK & START
Park in the village. Start from the post box.

THE VILLAGES
Ampney St Peter (pronounced Amney) has a single golden
grey street with a branch past the church. But wander about
yourself to see why many people think this is one of the
most attractive small villages in the Cotswolds; not a stone
out of place and complete harmony of style. It is one of a
trio of villages taking their names from the Ampney Brook,
which flows into the Thames. Try to get the Guide to the
United Parish of the Ampneys with Driffield and Poulton,
which has a charming primitive map and detailed notes on all
the churches. And make sure you give lots of money.

St Peter's is a tiny Saxon church with a distinctive
saddleback tower which has a sundial on the south wall. The
style of building, the methods and the scale seem wildly
different from most Cotswold churches, and so perhaps were
the motives. A pity about the heavy Victorian restoration.
More was in progress when we called, and the symbolism of
the tin of magnolia paint, which is an off white shade,
caused us some concern.

The walk visits Ampney St Mary which is even smaller. It once
stood by the brook near the main road (A417) but moved to
higher ground after the Black Death of 1349. The Norman
church was abandoned in the fields and decayed, but it was
restored in 1913. This is a plain and dignified little
church with an odd batter to the north wall of the nave and
south wall of the chancel. Go and examine the medieval wall

paintings. They are drawn in the usual browns and ochres and most are not very distinct, but the artist's talent is obvious. The faces have subtly different expressions of meekness or piety, and the lines of the clothing are lively and flowing. A leaflet tells us that the man on the left of the door is looking down the spoke of a wheel; we must confess we could not quite figure him out. There is a fine griffin on the lintel of the north door.

Since the walk is short and level you will not be too tired to walk about Ampney Crucis, the largest of the villages. An amazingly long street winds between stone garden walls. It has a park, two pubs and an old water mill. The church of the Holly Rood has colourful Victorian floor tiles which alone justify a visit. Look for the tattered copy of a mural showing poor St Erasmus being martyred. It is not quite clear what a torturer in hilarious winkle pickers is doing, but it does not look very nice. There is the massive and gloriously carved stone tomb of George Lloyd (1584), a sort of six poster with a colossal roof which might have inspired the Abbey National logo. There is a much praised 14th century cross in the churchyard. Its carved head was hidden in the staircase turret to prevent destruction by the Puritans, and not found until 1860.

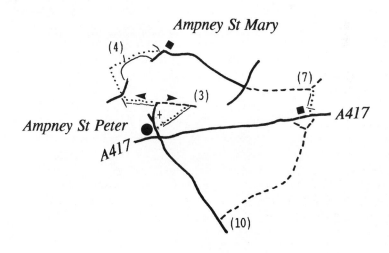

THE STROLL
A little wander of less than 1 mile. There is a fine avenue
of beech and sycamore trees and a view of the church set off
by a massive Cedar.

✳

(1) Face post box, go L to tiny green & fork R. Pass church R & rectory L, lane becomes track, to its end.

(2) Go R between trees to their end & take stile R just before wood.

(3) Follow fence on your L to field corner. Take 2 stiles & path back to start. ●

THE WALK

Some 4.5 miles on level paths, tracks and quiet lanes. This is a rich, level, farming landscape of hedgerows, distant woods and faintly whirring tractors; a complete contrast to most other walks in the book. You can look forward to a gem of a pocket sewage works. Some may prefer the Ampney Brook to which you can divert by three little bridges on the site of a long vanished mill. Even the smallest Cotswold rivers are clear, deep and fast. Here is a fascinating variety of water plants, especially in the more still and silted millpond.

✳

(1) Face post box, go L to tiny green & fork R. Pass church R & rectory L, lane becomes track, to its end.

(2) Go L via small gate & with hedge on your L, round field corner to gate & lane.

(3) Take stone stile opposite. Go to 2nd power pole from R. Turn 90deg R to join bending hedge & follow to cross bridge.

(4) Go with hedge on your R & keep same line over concrete bridge. Cross field diagonally [if wet, try round R edge] & take stile to lane.

(5) Go L, at phone box fork R, & on appx .5 mile to road.

(6) Take track opposite .4 mile to sharp L bend. ▲

◀(7) Take signposted stone stile R, then with hedge on your R to field corner & cross footbridge. Go ahead & pass house on your R to corner stile & A417.

(8) Go R appx 200yds to pass last house R. Cross road & take gate by London Rd sign.

(9) Follow concrete track past barns to junction. Go R appx 1 mile to lane.

(10) Go R appx .7 mile & cross A417 to start. ●

[Watch out for the neatly lawned, nautical looking sewage works with jaunty railings and interesting valves. "Danger", it warns - deep water and moving machinery. To see the Ampney Brook, take the stile L after the works.]

Bridge over the River Churn

Bagendon

WHERE
Map reference SP 012066, a tiny hamlet about half a mile
west of the A435 and three miles north of Cirencester.

PARK & START
Parking is very limited with the only space near the church.
If Bagendon is "full", don't spoil it, in this book we offer
lots of other villages. Start from the green by the church.

THE VILLAGE
Bagendon is the smallest village in this book. It has a
handful of mellow stone cottages, a water mill and a school
(now houses), a grand 18th century manor house, a church
and a war memorial. Sleeping on the north side of the little
valley of Perrotts Brook, a tributary of the River Churn,
there is little to suggest its distant past.

But in the 1950's Elsie Clifford, a local archaeologist,
excavated ditches and mounds around the village and established that it had been the main settlement of the Dobunni
people during the 1st century AD. Here they reared cattle,
cultivated the land using sophisticated ploughs, traded
widely and minted their own coins. Mrs Clifford's findings
can be seen in the Corinium Museum at Cirencester.

St Margaret's church with its saddleback tower is early
Norman and the churchyard has a Norman tomb. There are
fragments of 15th century stained glass. On the south face
of the tower is a scratch dial, or mass dial, with a few
radiating lines to show the times of the main services.

North of the village past the war memorial, lies the parkland
of Bagendon House. There are noble beeches with many of the
copper variety and fine horse chestnuts. Its woods are ideal
for wild flowers, with a spring carpet of bluebells.

You can link the Stroll (about 1.7 miles) and the Walk (3 miles) to form a longer circuit of 3.7 miles by diverting to the Walk after Para (6) as marked.

THE STROLL
Quite varied for an outing of only 1.7 miles, with a winding lane, a bit of a climb, a wood and a green track. See the note about linking it to the Walk.

(1) From tiny green by church take lane on R of No Through Road, appx .5 mile to sharp R bend at Butlers Cottage.

(2) Take corner gate. Note hedge R ends short of field bottom and head for it. Go up with hedge on your L to corner.

(3) Take small gate, then go R & thro wall, to face UPHILL with wall on your L. Go ahead 15yds & bear L on slightly banked path.

(4) Banks soon vanish; follow woodland path, bearing L to join path ◀

◀ *from R. Go on to join wide earth track. Follow L to meet wood edge track.*

(5) Take small gate opposite. Go ahead over CREST & (when you see it) make for power pole with yellow sign. Take field corner gate to lane.

(6) Go L appx 400yds, joining road, to end of wood R & small gate L.

To join Walk go on 25 yds & take stone stile R. Now read from Walk Para (2) point *.

(7) Take small gate L down field edge & keep same line to start. ●

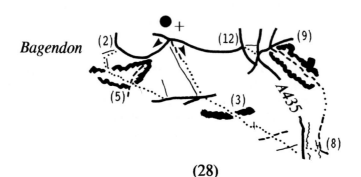

Bagendon

(28)

THE WALK

About 3 miles. This little tour of the neighbourhood takes you up from the Perrotts Brook and over the hill to the River Churn. Broad views from the top and a pleasant sight of the river. See the note about linking it to the Stroll.

✱

(1) From tiny green by church take No Through Road, becomes track then field edge path, appx .4 mile to lane.

[This is the Welsh Way, a drovers' road used to drive Welsh cattle and sheep into England. The upland sections have typically wide verges.]

*(2) Go L 25 paces & take stone stile R. * Turn half L & see line of trees opposite. Head for L end via 3 midfield stiles, & take stone stile into trees.*

(3) Cross trees to field. Go L & take field corner stile. Head for pole in opposite fence (R of bush) & take stile.

(4) Keep same line over field corner & cross drive via 2 stiles. Cross field diagonally & take corner gate. ◀

(5) Go down fence a few yds & take stile R thro cypresses. ◀ *[The shelter belt behind was a small mixed woodland and felt natural. Why does the golf club chose a geometrical line of Lawson's cypress which look as relevant in this landscape as a motor bike in an art gallery?] Head for R end of clubhouse, passing green hedge on your L & down to track. Go R a few paces & take gate to A435.*

(6) Go L to club entrance & take track opposite. Round L bend to end of wall & go R to cross bridge.

(7) Cross field passing power pole on your R, & take 2 gates opposite to track.

(8) Go L on track to its end, then keep same line to take wooden gate ahead.

(9) Go with hedge on your L & follow track appx .6 mile to lane. ▶

(29)

(10) Go L to A435. Cross to double poled electrical gizmo [with interesting tap on base] & take stile on L.

(11) Cross to 3 fingered post in far corner (via stiles & gate), & lane T junction.

(12) Take stem of T (Bagendon) appx .5 miles back to start.

[Some of the mounds which were part of the Dobunni settlement can be seen from the lane.]

St Margaret's Church, Bagendon

The Green at Little Barrington

(31)

The Barringtons

WHERE
Map reference SP 210137, neighbouring villages off the A40
between Northleach and Burford.

PARK & START
Park in the wide main street of Great Barrington. Start from
the war memorial.

THE VILLAGE
Near neighbours across the River Windrush, Great and Little
Barrington are so different in appearance and atmosphere that
they might be miles apart.

Great Barrington is a company town, more Crewe than Port
Sunlight. In grey stone with fawn tints, it lies on a single
level street at the west end of which are the gates of "the
Company", Barrington Park. This 18th century stately has
spacious grounds and a herd of fallow deer. Many of the
little estate workers' houses became very delapidated until
1977, when the District Council took action. Even now there
are a couple of near ruins, the last thing we had expected in
the Cotswolds. We would not have mentioned our impression
of bleak emptiness but for reading similar comments by
another writer.

Strong's Causeway links the villages and the Windrush rushes
and skids under it by two bridges. It was built in the 17th
century by Thomas Strong, local quarryman and master mason.
The Strongs built many noble Cotswold buildings and supplied
Christpher Wren with stone for St Paul's Cathedral.

Little Barrington clusters companionably round a deeply
sloping green which was once a quarry. A trickle of a stream
rises from a bed of rushes in the middle. There are the usual
comfortably spaced and friendly Cotswold cottages, all a

little different but at peace with each other and the landscape.

In Great Barrington church is memorial to Captain Edward Bray shows him in Tudor armour with his sword on the right side. You probably carry yours on the left. This clever gent was pardoned by Elizabeth I for a murder and vowed never again to draw a sword with his right hand.

Little Barrington's Norman church is small, plain and peaceful. There are some wall paintings.

The speed and volume of the Windrush must have shouted "power" to our grandfathers. There was a mill between the Barringtons which you pass on the Stroll, and another at Windrush which is on the Walk. Both are now private homes. A third mill at the northern tip of the walk is now in ruins. They give memorable views of the Windrush as it races out of Gloucestershire to Oxfordshire at Burford. There are a few hydraulic rams in the Cotswolds (see Chedworth) used for pumping water or generating electricity, but why does the river not shout to us?

The Walk visits the nearby village of Windrush where the houses huddle good naturedly round a triangular green with six lime trees. Go and see St Peter's church. The Norman doorway has a double row of sinister bulgy eyed and beaked heads which have glared crossly at the world for nine centuries.

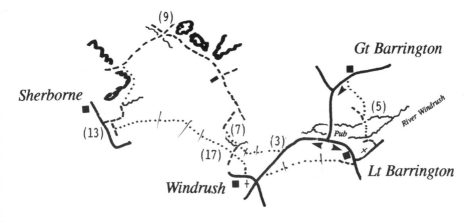

THE STROLL
A circuit of nearly 2 miles to visit both villages, both churches and the single pub. Mainly on lanes.

✱

(1) From war memorial take road DOWN, pass church & cross river to Fox Inn & road junction.

(2) Go L to Little Barrington, pass lane L & up to phone box.

(3) Take lane L, pass church, & take next lane L to its end. ◀

(4) Cross bridge R. Follow fenced path via bridge, & pass mill house on your L to gate & track.

(5) Take stile R. Bear L towards R end of buildings up to stile. Go L to big chimneyed Village Hall & take gate on its L to lane.

(6) Go R a few paces & take walled path L to main street. Go L to start. ●

THE WALK
About 7 miles in the valley of the River Windrush which you cross four times. There are willows, ditches and tiny streams and no real hills. Much of the walking is on tracks, with a few lanes. We were sad to miss a promising little sewage works on which construction was starting. You should have better luck.

✱

(1) From war memorial take road DOWN, pass church & cross river to Fox Inn & road junction.

(2) Go R (Windrush) appx 4 mile & pass road sign to sharp L bend.

(3) Take stone stile R. Go ahead making for R side ◀

of farm, & take stile in wall. Go parallel with wall on your L & down to cross stream.

(4) Turn half R & take stone stile into mill grounds. Go ahead to house, then R & ROUND it, to take stone stile. ▶

(34)

(5) Bear a little R to cross bridge & take gate. Go R with field edge & take corner gate.

(6) Go L via midfield gate. Keep same line to field edge gate & cross bridge.

(7) Go with hedge on your R to meet track by gate. Go L to farm, pass between barns towards house, & go R to gateway.

(8) Take track L with farm on your L appx .6 mile (past 1st wood R to end of 2nd), to track junction & young fingerpost.

(9) Go L past 2nd post & into trees. Go thro mill ruins & cross river bridge

(10) Take track ahead between trees appx .5 mile (crosses hedge), to double gates L near wood.

(11) Take gates L & go with wood on your R to cross stile. Cross field diagonally R to field corner gate & bridge.

(12) Follow track past works L, round R bend & appx 200yds to track L.

(13) Go L a few paces & take stile L. Go ahead parallel with wall L, & take stile by power pole.

(14) Go with hedge (later fence) on your R .5 mile, & take stile to open field

(15) NB 2 power poles ahead. Cross field to meet hedge 100 yds R of 2nd.

(16) Go with wall/hedge on your R, cross stone stile, pass barn on your R & down to cross brook.

(17) Head for R end of black barn ahead & take gate to track. Take stile opposite. Go with fence on your L, pass wooden stile L & go R to take stone one.

(18) Follow walled path, becomes lane, to phone box junction. [Windrush]

(19) Go L, pass church on your R to house No 27.

(20) Take kissing gate opposite & bear L. Go parallel with garden fences, then R between 2 trees & take gate.

(21) Go with wall on your L & keep same line appx 500yds (via stone stile & water trough, then midfield) to take wooden stile.

(22) Bear L to pass 50yds R of tree clump & take

stile. Bear R to gap between barns & take gate.

(23) Go L to lane & corner of green. Circle to pass phone box on your R. Follow lane back to Fox Inn & back to start.

Village Pump - Little Barrington

Bibury

WHERE
Map reference SP 116069. Village on B4425 (formerly A433)
seven miles north-east of Cirencester.

PARK & START
Riverside parking on B4425 and near bridge by Swan Hotel,
from where both the Stroll and Walk start.

THE VILLAGE
Bibury is built of golden brown and warm cream stone and lies
curled in the bottom of a deep valley. Almost a century ago
Willam Morris, poet, craftsman and social reformer, declared
it to be the finest village in England. Countless others
have praised it since and the visitors pour in, though many
go no further than the bridge, the trout farm, the Mill (now
a museum) and nearby Arlington Row. In fact there are two
villages, the Mill and houses nearby being in Arlington.

Both the Stroll and the Walk pass through Bibury village,
missed by many, where St Mary's Church and attractive
cottages lie in a peaceful backwater. And they pass the fast
clear weed trailing Coln where ducks dabble, coots and
moorhens parade their fluffy young, and astonishing big
brown trout flicker to and fro.

St Mary's church has Saxon origins, and like most churches,
has been extended century by century. The nave was
lengthened, new ailes added, windows fitted, the chancel roof
replaced, and the tower raised. Wealth from the wool trade
did not reach the Cotswolds until after the period of the
Black Death in the mid 1300's, and most churches were
therefore extended and embellished in the Norman period and
the late 1300's. However the large and elaborate windows in
the north wall are in the Decorated style (1250 - 1400). Go
and have a look and get the excellent booklet.

Arlington Row

Dry-stone waller near Bibury

(38)

Returning to the connection with William Morris, you may remember the "arts and crafts" series of stamps issued for Christmas 1992. The 24p stamp was a detail from a stained glass window in the north chancel by Karl Parsons (1884 -1934).

St Mary's churchyard is mellow and fitting, with delightfully carved gravestones in local stone and no black marble with silver angles. There are great stone boxes with fat lids and some "bale tombs", which have two or more cylinders of stone on top to represent bolts of cloth. The parishoners should also be proud of their standard roses.

The trout farm started in 1902 on an old watercress farm. It rears fish for the kitchen and for restocking fishing waters, which tend to get depleted by anglers and to suffer from pollution. Until 1976 the farm raised only the native brown trout, but the droughts of this period wiped out their stocks which were replaced by the North American rainbow trout. However you can see the brownies lurking in the River Coln, where they seem to benefit from food parcels from the yanks upstream.

Both Walk and Stroll pass much photographed Arlington Row, the enchanting huddle of 15th century weavers' cottages which stand by the so called Rack Isle, where cloth was put out to dry. Now, say the National Trust signs, it is where mallards nest.

THE STROLL
About 1.5 miles, with the village, the cricket ground, an awesome row of beech trees and Arlington Row.

✱

(1) From Swan Hotel follow pavement with river on R. At fork go R thro village & back to B4425.

◄

◄(2) Go R past 1st R & take 2nd (Coln St Aldwyns). Go on a few yards & take lane R. Cross bridge, bear R thro buildings & curve up, past small round building L, to gateway on lane.

►

(3) Go R on track & take small gate. Bear R, follow WALL past cricket ground L, & take stone stile in wall corner into wood.

(4) Follow wood path to far edge, swing R & down steps past backs of houses, then via stile to lane.

(5) Go L past houses [Arlington Row]. At end of row go R via bridge, to road & start. ●

[These towering beeches are about the biggest on these walks. Similarly the black M&S underpants size 38/40 seen hanging in the tree by the pavilion.]

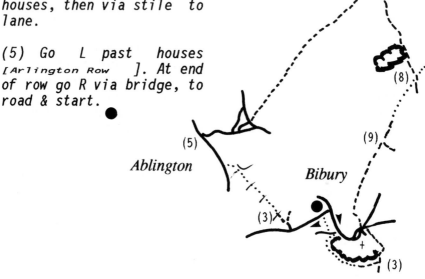

Ablington

Bibury

THE WALK
Some 5 miles of field paths and tracks. You visit the hamlet of Ablington with its elegant Manor House glimpsed over a high wall. This was the home of J Arthur Gibbs, a young squire whose book A Cotswold Village" published shortly before his death in 1898, is a classic of rural literature.

There is a stretch across one of the high bare plateaus of the Cotswolds, illustrating the contast between these uplands and the sheltered valleys.

✳

(1) From bridge by Swan Hotel take Cirencester road. Pass Mill R & on 500yds to phone box opposite "No Through Road".

(2) Take lane R & thro 5 bar gate to track. Fork L to last house.

(3) Take stone stile & follow field edge. Keep same line via stiles to wall & wooden gate ahead.

(4) Bear L & pass house on your L to lane. Go R 500yds down to fork.

(5) Go R, cross river, pass L fork, & take next lane L to road junction, (L side).

(6) Take stone track opposite (becomes grass track) for appx 1.5 miles, to approach farm buildings.

[A long track between broad stoney fields where the only sounds under the sky are distant rooks. The main farm building is "Saltway Barn" which suggests the origins of the route.] ◀

(7) Bear R, pass gate by brick shed & take gate by buildings. Take track R .6 mile & pass wood R to next wall. Take gate.

(8) Go R with wall past barn R, then on track to gate & junction. [See the fuzzy shooting butts grouped round a dry pond.]

(9) Go R, pass square grass hump L & follow track to B4425.

[Future anthropologists will excavate these mysterious hill top mounds and wonder at the strange moist chambers and pipeworks.]

(10) Go R & take wall gap by phone box. Go thro village & rejoin B4425. Take bridge L to end of cottages, then go R back to start.●

Bisley

Map reference SO 905060, a village about four miles east of
Stroud. It is easiest reached from Chalford on the A419
between Stroud and Cirencester, from where is is signposted
to the north.

PARK & START
By the pavement near the Bear Inn.

THE VILLAGE
Bisley is a large village with much to see, which perches on
a summit surrounded by deep valleys and combes. The high
point at about 250 metres is the church spire, used as a
landmark by World War II pilots. First seen as you approach
from Chalford is a cluster of houses ranged around the end of
a combe. There are four or five narrow streets which run up
and down and from side to side, grey brown roofs sit at all
angles, the houses face this way and that, yet with hardly a
straight line it is all a comfortable unity.

Like most Cotswold villages, Bisley owes much of its
charm to the prosperity of the wool trade. Scattered closely
over the hillside to form an amphitheatre are fine cream and
grey merchants' houses and trim weavers' cottages. On the
crest is a handsome church and nearby a quaint early 19th
century lock up. Seven wells present their waters through an
ecclesiatical looking range of gabled spouts and troughs.
They are dressed on Ascension Day like those in the
Derbyshire Peak District, with flowers and leaves.

Bisley is also home to an incredible legend known as the
Bisley Boy. The story goes that at the age of ten the future
Queen Elizabeth I went to stay with the gentry living in Over
Court, one of the village's fine houses. She was taken ill
with the plague and died. Terrified that they might in some

way be blamed for her death, the villagers replaced the princess with John Neville, a local lad supposed to look very like the young Elizabeth. This accounts, the tale goes, for the "Queen" remaining virgin all her days. The story seems to have been, well - created, by a Victorian rector, Canon Keble, after discovery of a young girl's skeleton in the grounds of Over Court.

All Saints' church stands on a site which saw Roman pagan rituals and later a Saxon church. The modern church is very lofty and spacious with a cheerfully glowing east window and a ring of eight bells. The Norman font is delicately carved with a rope pattern and lilies and two fish in the bowl; the stem is recent but what a skilled match. In fact the whole church was restored in 1862 by Canon Keble, so as the booklet describing the church rightly points out, you will find no pure Saxon, Norman or pure anything else. All Saints' was not built as a museum, but like a house or farm, was repaired and modernised from time to time when there was cash.

The Wells, Bisley.

In the churchyard the yews are tall rather than the usual squat and humble shrubs, demonstrating that it is a woodland tree and can grow to some 80 feet. Near the church wall are small brass memorial plaques which may be because burials ceased in about 1900 in favour of a new cemetery on the edge of the village.

You cannot miss a rather careworn hexagonal monument topped by a wheel cross. This is "The Bonehouse", local name for the unique "poor soul's light". It was used to hold candles during masses for the poor before the Reformation. In fact it is the head of a well which was capped in the 12th century. It seems that one night the priest never reached a dying parishoner, and that later the reverend corpse was found in the well. The Pope is supposed to have ordered that the momument be built, and to punish the parishioners forbad burials at Bisley for two years, during which the dead had to be carried eighteen miles to Bibury.

The Bear Inn was once the court house and the upper floor is supported by iron columns. The other pub is the Stirrup Cup, the sign depicting a jolly gent in a red coat who looks as though he might also need some support.

THE STROLL
About 1.5 miles on paths and lanes. You visit the churchyard, walk up an ancient track worn between banks, and return through the village.

Follow Walk
Paras (1) to (4).

(4a) Go   L   to   road
junction.   Go   L   a   few
paces & take path R.

- THEN, follow Walk
Paras (13) to end.
●

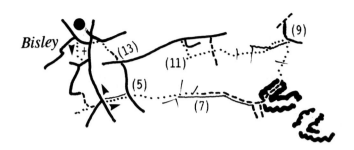

THE WALK

About 4 miles which includes most of the Stroll. Heading east from the village you walk remote hedged tracks, pass a little wood and quite suddenly meet a deep combe. Much of the walk back follows a lively little stream, clear and fast like all its Cotswold siblings.

✳

(1) Face Bear Inn & go L, take kissing gate & thro playground to churchyard. Go with wall on your R to far end & take steps to lane. [Wells on the L.]

(2) Go R, pass lane R & rising path R. Curve L down past footpath R & curve L again to cross stream.

(3) Follow path appx 450 yds up to road junction.

(4) Take gate opposite & go with hedge on your L via 2 small gates to lane.

(5) Take gate opposite & pass barns on your L. Head for FAR R field corner & take small gate.

(6) Go with hedge/wall/ fence on your R via small gates appx 500yds, to join hedged track.

(7) Follow down past track R to T junction at wood. Go L appx 600yds to track end at stile & gate.

[Walkers must on no account try the jumps in this field.]

(8) Go AHEAD via gate below, & down field track to gate/stile & track ▶

▲

(9) Cross stream & go L a few paces to take stile L. Go with stream on your L via 3 small fields & cross bridge.

(10) Go with stream on your R via stiles. Pass houses R & on to appx 50 yds from field end & markpost L.

[Here the stream plonks and chuckles through the grass.] ◢

(11) Go R over stream & up, curving L from track R to field top stile & track.

(12) Go L to road bend (Bisley /Sapperton sign). Go on a few paces & take track R.

(13) Follow to end & take kissing gate. Keep same line over field to lane,

(14) Bear L between walls & down to lane. Take steps opposite down to street. Go L, lane R leads back to start.●

Bisley at all angles

Blockley

WHERE
Map reference SP 164350, a village midway between Moreton in Marsh and Chipping Campden on the B4479.

PARK & START
The village roads are not very wide and parking space is limited. There are places opposite the Post Office Stores, but if you park elsewhere use special care not to get in the way of villagers.

Both Stroll and Walk start from the Post Office Stores.

THE VILLAGE
Blockley is a steeply sloping hillside village by the fast flowing Blockley Brook, and the fine bowling green is said to be the only level ground. It looks across the valley to the vast flank of a hill, green and gently folded with a fringe of trees on the crest. The houses were built between the 16th and 19th centuries in a stone which varies from powerful ginger to pale cream.

The village once boasted twelve corn mills which in the 1700's were converted to silk throwing. The water contained enough lime to give a fine sheen to the washed yarn, which was sold to the Coventry ribbon weavers. The mills worked until the local trade was ruined by foreign competition in the late 1900's. Now they are fine houses, and with the rows of former silk workers cottages, give Blockley a slightly un-Cotswold look.

The flowing stream brought other benefits, for in the 1880's a dammed mill pond ran a dynamo to produce electric light, making Blockley one of the first villages in the country to have it.

The church of St Peter and St Paul has Saxon origins, there was a Saxon burial ground under the top of the High Street. The earliest surviving work is Norman (1180) but there are records of a monastic community in 855, established to convert pagans in the wild North Cotswolds. The church holds a rich array of monuments, brasses, busts, effigies and marble tablets, chiefly in memory of members of local landowning families. The handsome square tower has four little turrets embellished with crockets and four golden weather vanes, not uncommon in the Cotswolds.

Civic pride in Blockley is strong; see the discs marking such lost features as the sites of the stocks and the fairground.

Two cottages are worth searching for. Rock Cottage was the home between 1804 and 1814 of the prophetess Joanna Southcott. This Devon farmer's daughter and domestic servant uttered mystical incantations predicting vague catastrophe to the many, and a misty Utopia for the saved. From the 1790's for some fifteen years was an age of such prophets, attributed by the historian EP Thompson to popular frustration of a longing for political revolution in Britain. Joanna was by far the greatest of them, and her cult survived in various forms until the end of the 1900's. Fish Cottage on the High Street has a memorial board to a tame trout which lived twenty years in a garden pool and ate from the hand of its owner, William Keyte.

THE STROLL An easy 1 mile wander through the village and around the outside on lanes and field paths. Mud.

(1) At Post Office Stores face church & go R up Bell Lane to junction, then R up Bell Bank to T junction. ▼

(2) Take stile on R of house ahead. Follow L edge of field, round L corner & on appx 400yds to round next corner, & take gate to lane end. ▶

(3) Follow lane to T junction. Go R appx 50 yds & take path L between houses, cross stream & up to junction.

(4) Go L & along stream, then up to road. Go R to start.

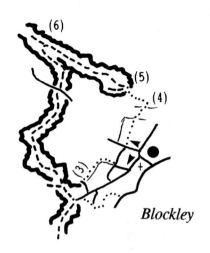

Blockley

Blockley in Autumn

THE WALK

About 3.5 miles. There is a gorgeous deep, green valley with wooded sides , but most of the walking is on tracks in narrow strips of valley woodland.

(1) From Post Office Stores face church & go L. Pass road R & take road L to junction with lane L.

(2) Take stile R & go ahead midfield, to hedge gap by last tree of row.

(3) Bear R over next field & cross stile (if obstructed, go 50yds R & take path L). Bear L to 5th tree from R (topless).

(4) Look up valley to NEAREST CORNER of wood on OPPOSITE slope, & sight gate. Cross to it & enter.

(5) Take R of 2 tracks 1 mile to track junction.

(6) Take 2nd track L appx 4 mile to road

(7) Take small gate opposite & follow main track appx 1 mile to house, gate & lane.

(8) Go ahead appx 300yds to road. [Track R gives 1.25 miles (each way) stroll in Bourton Woods.]

(9) Go L to start.

Blockley Churchyard

Broadway

WHERE
WHERE
Map reference SP 094375, a village between Evesham and
Moreton in Marsh on the A44.

PARK & START
There are paying car parks on the east side of the village
(Leamington Road) and the west (Snowshill Road). Leamington
Road is cheaper and unlimited in time, whilst Snowshill Road
allows up to four hours.

We start two Walks and the Stroll from the War Memorial on
the green at the west end, but the east end park is en route
the Stroll and Walk (B).

THE VILLAGE
Broadway is a Cotswold showplace, the most famous village in
England ranged lazily along the "broad-way" (the A44). In all
sizes and shapes, with frontages wandering back and forth,
are almost half a mile of honey and grey buildings, hotels,
pubs, boutiques, tea shops, bookshops, antique shops and
houses. They are more varied than in many Cotswold villages,
for Broadway's position on the edge of the Vale of Evesham
has brought in some thatch and timber framing. In spite of
crowded popularity and manicured neatness, it is beautiful,
and its history of catering for visitors runs back to when
twenty of the hotels and pubs were coaching inns on the main
London - Worcester road.

Get a guide book locally for details of interesting places,
but look out for; (a) Abbots Grange, the 14th century former
residence of the Abbot of Pershore, which is by the green;
(b) Prior's Manse, also 14th century and on the main street;
(c) The Lygon Arms, built in 1620 and formerly the White
Hart, also on the main street.

On the Stroll and Walk (B) you can see the "Old Church". St Eadburgha's which is 12th century. It was abandoned as the parish church in 1832, and a new one built near the village. There are Norman columns, a carved oak panel of the Apostles and the last of Sir Thomas Phillipps, a book collector.

On Walk (A) are two interesting villages. Childswickham is an appealing mix of Cotswold stone, timber framed and mellow red brick houses. The Norman church is quite small but has a handsome ribbed 15th century spire.

Buckland is a tiny single street village with the Early English style church of St Michael. In the south ailse are some medieval cream and buff encaustic floor tiles. The brown and gold ones are the Victorian version of the same product. The east window and fragments in the south window are 15th century. The other glass is rather distinguished Victorian work of 1883 by William Morris. There are fine carved pews and a mighty little organ perched on a gallery supported by tapered wooden piers.

Broadway is likely to be a popular starting point so we have provided a Stroll and two Walks. They form a contrast which we think shows both sides of the Cotswolds. Walk (A) is levelish and touches the broad and arable Vale of Evesham. Walk (B) climbs through woodland and hill farming country to Broadway Hill, one of the highest points in the Cotswolds.

Childswickham

(52)

THE STROLL

About 1.75 miles on fields and lanes. A level route on which the main feature is St Eadburgha's Church, about .75 mile south of the village. Walk (B) follows this route as far as para (3).

✳

(1) At War Memorial face Cotswold Court centre & go L on main street to Horse & Hound

[Go left to see St Eadburgha's church, small and square in a tidal wave of gravestones.]

(2) Take path R (Old Church), keep same line by iron fence R & take stile. Go on to cross stiles by stream, & on one field to take next stile.

(3) Bear L to small lone oak & take stile. Bear R past projecting hedge corner & big oak to gate & road. ◀

(4) Go R to 1st house & take lane L. Go appx 600yds to pass houses R, & take stile R.

(5) Go with fence on your R, cross stiles & stream. Bear L to cross bridge, then up to church to field corner gate, drive & road. Go L to start. ●

WALK (A)

About 6 miles on field paths and tracks in the Vale of Evesham. There is a fine green lane, market gardens, high hedges, a disused railway, a church with medieval tiles and a climb onto the hills giving wide views.

✳

(1) From War Memorial pass Swan Inn & take "No Through Road" (China Sq). Follow grass track .75 mile to rail bridge. ▶

[The Norway spruce in the wood seems to have been thinned but is still dark and sad. This fertile clay will grow better woods, but not so fast.

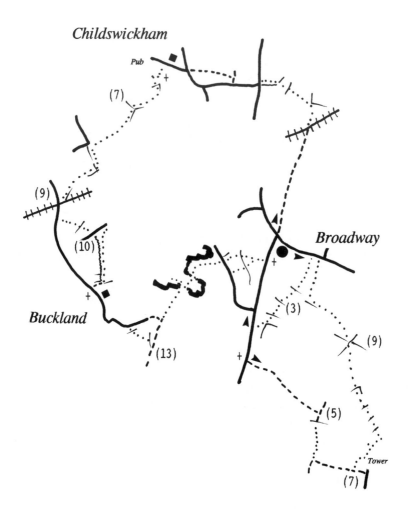

Childswickham

Pub

(7)

(9)

(10)

Buckland

(13)

Broadway

(3)

(9)

(5)

Tower

(7)

(54)

(2) Go on via stile for one field & take stile L. Go diagonally R to gap on L of wood & cross stile & bridge.

(3) Go to midhedge stile by power pole & tree. Cross, & with hedge on your L to stile & A44.

[Against the hills ahead the village spreads around the steeple amongst small fields of prosperous vegetables. It should be painted.]

(4) Take lane opposite 250yds to foot of slope & take track R. Go 45 paces & take grass track L, thro plots to road

(5) Take "No Through Road" opposite, pass track R, to end of lane. Go L & cross bridge to churchyard.

(6) Pass tower on your L & take kissing gate. Go ahead via 2 stiles to field. Go L round field edge to exact opposite point. Duck under fallen willow to next field.

(7) Go L on field edge to end of tall hedge, then on same line with gappy hedge to lane bend, DON'T TAKE LANE.

(8) Go L (hedge on your R) & take stile R. Cross slab bridge & go with hedge on your L. Round bends & take stile L to stile & lane by rail bridge.

(9) Go L appx 250yds & opposite Little Buckland House, take gate L. Go ahead & take gate, & keep same line to stile & lane.

[What a sudden change from fertile flatlands to rough grazing as we leave the Vale of Evesham for the hills.]

(10) Go L appx 150yds to power pole with gizmo R, & take stile R. Bear R with stream on your R & take gate. Go on with stream, then wooden fence, & take corner stile R.

(11) Go ahead via small gate to lane & on to T junction. Go L thro village, pass church, round L bend, & pass ponds to last house L.

(12) Take stile R, then next, & follow grass track up L to stile in top fence. Go R to stile & track.

(13) Go L to L bend by barns. Take twin stiles R & next one, to field corner. Go L on field edge, take 2 gates & keep same line down to small gate & wood.

(14) Go down R a few yards, curve L & on 20 paces to take path down R, to small gate & field. Go with hedge on your L then via fenced path to road.

(15) Take stile opposite & head for church. Take stiles & kissing gate to drive & road. Go L to start.

WALK (B)

About 5 miles of field paths and tracks climbing from the village, at 90 metres, through glorious woodland to the Broadway Tower at 313 metres. The views are astounding.

Follow Stroll to para (3)

(4) Pass St Eadburgha's on your R & take gateway & track L. Follow (ignore R fork) appx .6 mile to T junction of tracks.

(5) Go R & take gate. Bear up L to pass front of house & join track to gateway, DON'T TAKE IT.

(6) Go L & past houses to join lane at bend. Keep same line appx 300yds to gate, & take stile L.

(7) Go ahead bearing R to pass ladder stile R & take track. Pass buildings R & take small gate L to Tower.

(56)

[Four lanky castellated towers crowd round a square bit with Georgian windows and stone balconies. A slightly cockeyed door sits between the tower bases, which are splayed like feet. This wacky edifice was built in 1799 and a plaque tells you all about it. We need more of these.

Nearby are highland cattle and red deer in the Broadway Tower Country Park, and little combes and knolls of a curious miniature landscape. At your feet the ground plunges into the Vale of Evesham.]

(8) Pass Tower heading for lower field corner & take stile. Follow straight clear path (Cotswold Way) via stiles to Clumps Farm sign.

(9) Bear R with path & take bottom midhedge stile, then ahead down old hedge & take stile. Bear R & continue on Cotswold Way to emerge opposite Leamington Road.

(10) Go L to start.

The Steps of St Eadburgha's Church

Bourton on the Water

WHERE
Map reference SP 168206. Village about three miles south of
Stow on the Wold.

PARK & START
There are pay car parks at each end of the village, the one
off Station Road is cheaper for a longer stay. Elsewhere
there is limited free parking.

Both Walk and Stroll start from the War Memorial in the main
street.

THE VILLAGE
Bourton on the Water is one of the best known Cotswold
villages and has an exceptional history. We are not going to
enter any murderous controversy about which is the prettiest
village, but Bourton is in the squad.

Before the Romans came there was a British Camp known as
Salmonsbury; you can see its scanty remains on the Stroll,
cunningly camouflaged as a bed of nettles to fool the Romans.
They had an important settlement by their Fosse Way, now the
A429 (ACCCCXXIX). There was a posting house, a religious
shrine and a sort of transport cafe, all of which were
excavated after World War II.

Modern Bourton has pubs, gift shops, teashops, restaurants, a
motor museum, a perfumery, a village life exhibition, a model
railway and a birdland. Behind the Old New Inn there is a
model village which is a one ninth scale replica of Bourton
built by local craftsmen in the 1930's. If none of these
attractions appeals to you, copy most visitors and just walk
about enjoying the the honey coloured houses and delicate
18th century bridges over the little river. Make sure, as in
all the villages, that you visit the church. Bourton's is

dedicated to St Lawrence and has a 14th century chancel and Georgian tower. All this is obviously calculated to keep people in the village and leave the countryside free for us.

"On the Water" refers to the clear, swift River Windrush which hurries through the middle of the village spanned by little stone bridges. Since the 1970's a series of lakes has been created from worked out gravel pits to the south and east of the Village. The bankside paths are pleasant walks with scope for bird watching - mute swans, canada geese, grebes, coots, gulls, herons, all manner of ducks and occasionally a kingfisher. Bourton has rightly been called "The Venice of the Cotswolds".

Several Long Distance Footpaths run from Bourton on the Water. The Heart of England Way will take you north for 100 miles to Cannock Chase, The Oxfordshire Way runs 65 miles south east to Henley on Thames, The Wardens Way and Windrush Way are local Cotswold routes.

The Bridges of Bourton

THE STROLL

A 2 mile wander on fieldpaths and tracks with lakes and the undistinguished remains of the Salmonsbury British camp. The lakes are calmly lovely - clear and rippling with small bushy islands, fringed with green reeds and dotted with black diving coots. There is an enjoyable quantity of mud in damp weather, for those who like that sort of thing; a welly walk.

(1) From War Memorial follow main street past 2 stone bridges to end. Take Station Street L.

(2) Go appx 100yds & take footpath R, appx 300yds to T junction with surfaced path. Go L to R bend & take stile L.

(3) Follow path via bends to stile & lane. Go R 500yds, over crosspath, to L bend with houses ahead.

(4) Continue L to 2 gates & take gap by R one. Pass path R, follow track to 3 gates & take stile by centre one.

(5) Bear L to walk with lake on your R to its corner. Keep same line & take stile ahead. Take bridge & follow wood path, bearing R along edge of trees to exit at stile to field.

(6) Bear L (check L) then go parallel with wood. [Salmonsbury Camp was the dull little mound R] Take 2 stiles & go to 3rd. DON'T TAKE IT.

(7) Go R via hedge gap & follow fenced path L (via field corner) to farm.

(8) Go ahead thro farm & take drive to lane. Go R a few yards to Station Road. Go L back to start.

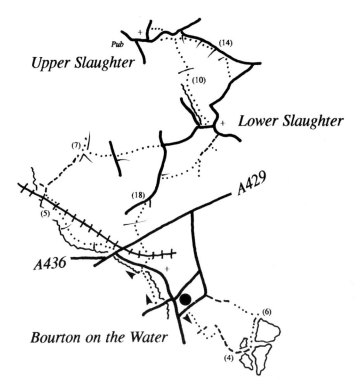

Upper Slaughter

Pub

(14)

(10)

Lower Slaughter

(7)

(18)

A429

(5)

A436

Bourton on the Water

(6)

(4)

Upper Slaughter

(61)

THE WALK

About 6 miles of fieldpaths and tracks with a few lanes; be prepared for the bridleways to be squelchy. The route follows the valley of the River Windrush with lines of willows and a circular pond full of weed. You walk over the broad dome of a hill with fine views and visit the little grey clusters of Lower Slaughter and Upper Slaughter.

These villages are as lovely and almost as much visited as Bourton. Lower Slaughter has little rivers and bridges and two prominent hotels. It is immaculate and personable, like an hotelier presenting his professional face. Upper Slaughter is a complete contrast, very small and spread casually over a hill and a little valley. It was was the home of the Victorian diarist Francis Witts whose elaborate mausoleum is in the church. Look out for the ground of the terrifyingly named Slaughters United Cricket Club.

(1) From War Memorial in main street, cross bridge & pass Duke of Wellington pub to fork by restaurant.

(2) Take signed footpath R thro houses, & cross field to join river. Follow upstream appx 300yds to cross bridge.

(3) Follow path to road. Go L by river to A429.

(4) Cross to R of bridge & take stile L of gate. Cross field parallel with river & take small steel gate. Go with fence on your L & take small gate.

(5) Follow railway 100yds, then bear R & follow edge of trees. Then with fence on your R, curve R & down to T junction of paths.

(6) Go R via gate (i) & field edge path to gate (ii). Go appx 75yds & take small gate R.

(7) Follow line of wall on your R to cross midfield to big tree clump. Take gate to lane, then track opposite to lane junction.

(8) Take lane opposite down to T junction. Cross bridge opposite, go L past mill & take 1st path L.

(62)

[On the kissing gate you may see a sad little brass plate, "Prince Charles - Lady Diane 27th July 1981".]

(9) Follow riverside path to end of fence, pass path L & bear R to take gate.

(10) Cross field & take hedge gap, then ahead to far field end & take stile. Keep same line, take stile & bridge & follow path to lane.

(11) Go L to village. Bear R to pass PHONEBOX & down to ford. Cross bridge & take stile R. Follow stream to lane junction.

[These trout do not respond to hummed snatches of Schubert's famous quintet. Please report if you have any luck with aquatic works by eg Handel, Smetana, Britten or Elgar.]

(12) Go R & up to take path L (again) & cross bridge.

(13) Bear up L with power lines & take gateway ahead. Keep same line to next gate & on, bearing L to corner stile & lane.

(14) Go R appx 150yds & take stile R. Take 2nd stile, keep same line to white gate & exit to lane.

(15) Go R, round L bend, pass road R & church L, to junction.

(16) Go L 100yds & take track R by river 300yds to gate.

(17) Bear R & go up with hedge on your R to small gate & lane. Go L appx 250yds & take stile L

[At this point you may admire a monumental pile of manure.]

(18) Cross field down to far edge of wood. Take stiles & cross field to A429.

(19) Take stile opposite & go on to cross railway embankment by fenced path.

[To stop you from spying on the embankment?]

(20) At fork go R to main street & L back to start.

Chedworth   Photo Judith Goodman

Chedworth

Map reference SP 052122. Village off A429 four miles south
west of Northleach.

PARK & START
Park by the church which is on the lane opposite the Three
Tuns pub, but not during services and therefore not on Sunday
mornings. Please check in the church porch for extra
services.

The alternative is on the wider verges of the road to the
village from the north side, near the gate of Manor Farm.
(See sketch map) If you park here, take the stile by the farm
gate and follow the path to the church, from which both the
Walk and Stroll start.

THE VILLAGE
The little cream, gold and grey stone houses and farms of
this big straggling village are sprinkled over the upper
slopes of a tributary valley of the River Coln. And there
are such trees and hedges and bursting gardens that from
above it seems lost in blossom, leaves and branches.

The Seven Tuns Inn bears the date 1610, but it is hard to
imagine that the village was dry before someone had the
brilliant idea of a pub. Now it is a free house and serves
meals which you can eat outside on tables under a tree.
Queen Street commemorates a visit to her aunts in 1491 by
Elizabeth of York, wife of Henry VII. This is the last royal
visit they can remember.

St Andrews church is small, simple and old. Parts of the
building and the tub shaped font are Norman from about 1100,
clear lofty windows in the south wall of the nave are of the
Perpendicular period (1350 - 1500). A "Breeches Bible" is

displayed in a glass case. This edition was in official use until the Authorised Version of 1611 and is named for its translation of Genesis III v 17, "they sewed fig leaves together and made themselves breeches". (What did we expect, jeans?) There is also a gorgeously decorated little organ, a fine 15th century wine glass pulpit and some gargoyles. St Andrews is one of a group of five jointly run churches.

The famous Roman Villa (National Trust) in the nearby woods which is named after the village is some distance away, but the Walk passes by. In 1864 a gamekeeper noticed that rabbits had dug up some loose mosaic and full excavation started the same year. Laid out for you are all the essentials of a Roman country house of the 2nd century, with living rooms, latrine, dining room and courtyards. There is also an elaborate suite of baths which you could use to demonstrate the delights of regular bathing to your children.

Back route to the Church   Photo Judith Goodman

(66)

Both Walk and Stroll meet the viaduct which from 1891 to 1961 carried a single track line of the Midlands & South Western Junction Railway between Andoversford and Cirencester. It seems that it was an important supply line during the build up of troops for D-day in 1944.

The Walk runs through the magnificent Chedworth Woods, a healthy mix of species of deciduous trees and conifers which is home to tits, woodpeckers, nuthatches, buzzards, wood anemones (we are onto flowers now), wood sorrel, honeysuckle and bluebells. John saw three fallow deer, which though they passed quickly, seemed to be small does of the dark type.

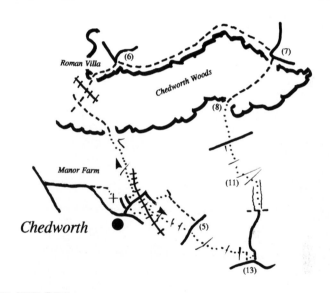

THE STROLL
An amble of about 1.5 miles on footpaths and lanes, with stepping stones and orchards.

*
(1) From church gate take path opposite down to lane & pub. ➤

(2) Go L appx 200 yds to foot of slope & take dead end lane R ➤

(67)

(3) Go appx 100 yds to near row of cottages L. Take steep path down R to cross stream & stile. [The water makes that deep plonking noise.]

(4) Go L & take field end stile. Go with stream on your L & take stile ahead, then keep same line via 2 stiles & wood to lane.

(5) Go L, at fork go L, & up to 2nd house L. Take stone track L

(6) Follow via small gate, stile, then gate, to end of lane. DON'T FOLLOW. Bear R on grass track, take stile, & on appx 15 yds to end of fence L to take gate.

(7) Go to bottom L corner gate & lane. Go L to T junction & L back to start. ●

THE WALK

In about 5 miles there are the magnificent sweeping contours of limestone country, a plunge through a deep green wood, an old railway, the Roman Villa, an avenue of colossal trees, and miles of treetops. Gentle climbs (and falls) on paths and lane.

✳

(1) Face church front & go R. Pass R fork & on to lane end, to take stile.

(2) Go with wall on your L, then ahead past bent tree & cross midfield to take stile by leaning tree

(3) Take steps to crest, then ahead via small gate. Keep same line over hill & down to stile & wood.

[A great whale back of a hill between two deep valleys, very typical of the Cotswolds.]

(4) Follow wide main path, pass fork R (by fence end), then 2 forks L, & drop to cross tracks. ◢

[The hazel has been coppiced to grow millions of young shoots forming a green tunnel. The trees that look like garden cypressus are actually western red cedar. There are some Norway spruce, and craggy oaks in a healthy and varied wood.]

◀ *(5) Go down R, under old rail bridge, pass Villa L, & on lane 300 yds to foot of slope & T junction.*

(6) Go R on stone track 1.25 miles to house & bend of road.

[Look for trees; wellingtonia (red bark), a very big once coppiced beech on the right, vast trunky poplars waiting to shed branches as you pass. Even Norway spruce can look impressive if they are big enough.]

(7) Go ahead appx 40 yds & take stile R. Follow wood path via yellow arrows:
- cross a path
- join earth track from L
- go 50 yds then down L
*   to earth track*
& follow up to wood edge.

(8) Go diagonally up to furthest lone oak, & on to road

▶

(69)

(9) Take stile opposite & cross midfield to LOWEST point in hedge AHEAD. Take path thro hedge to grass track.

(10) Go down L to valley bottom with old wall R. Go ahead 25 paces & take small path L, thro trees to stile & field.

(11) Go diagonally L & take hedge stile, & on same line to & take wall stile. Go R on grass track (narrow field) to gates & crosstracks.

(12) Take track ahead thro farm & down to cross valley. Rise round bends, pass grit box & Old Oak Cottage to take grass path R.

(13) Follow to stile & lane. Go R appx 30 yds past Saffron Hill, take grass path down R & take stile L.

(14) Cross midfield via 2 gates & take stile. Keep same line bearing closer to stream & take stile. Same line again to white gate & lane.

(15) Go down R to cottage & take path L. Go thro conifers & with stream on your R 4 fields. In 5th bear L & take far L corner stile.

(16) Cross bank & take stile. Go R & take stile, then bear L round curve to field end to stile. Go ahead to drive then R via gateway to start.

Coberley

WHERE
Map reference SP 963160. A village west of the A435, about four and a half miles south of Cheltenham.

PARK & START
Take the lane on the right of the Post Office past the stone cross to the village car park. Start from here.

THE VILLAGE
Coberley (pronounced Cubberley) is a modest cluster of cream and grey houses which lies on a slope by the River Churn, a mile downstream from its source at Seven Springs. On the green is a curious column with a sort of square stone lantern. The village still has a Post Office, a phone box and a school. Coberley won the Bledisloe Cup for the best kept village in 1989, 91 and 92.

The Seven Springs are claimed to be the source of the River Thames, in that they are the headwater furthest from the mouth. However, supporters of the River Churn are opposed by advocates for the Coln and the Windrush.

The main attraction is St Giles church, but few village churches can be hidden like this. On the lane to the A435 is an archway, which a sign directs you to enter (note the carved head above), then keep on to the churchyard. The entrance is around the back opposite the high wall of what was once Coberley Hall. This was the home of Dick Whittington long before he set off to London with the cat.

His mother, Lady Joan, was wife of Sir Thomas Berkeley who fought in the Battle of Crecy, and their tomb is in the church. Another Berkeley tomb is that of Sir Giles, whose heart is buried here but his body in Malvern, the only heart burial in the Cotswolds.

In medieval England important people might bequeath such personal momentoes to different churches and abbeys. The corpse was boiled in wine until soft, then shared out. We do not know if this can still be arranged, but if you are important you could find out. The churchyard has a memorial to Lombard, Sir Giles favourite horse. It is also a seat of *porcellionides pruinosus*, an uncommon woodlouse. The church porch is modern but has an engaging stained glass window of grapes and vine leaves, a 1990 memorial to Alan Beer.

The walk passes through the village of Cowley, where chunky grey Cowley Manor was the home of Sir James Horlick who invented the famous bedtime drink. Look for his initials on the gables of some houses and barns. Look also at the bogus bell on the old schoolhouse.

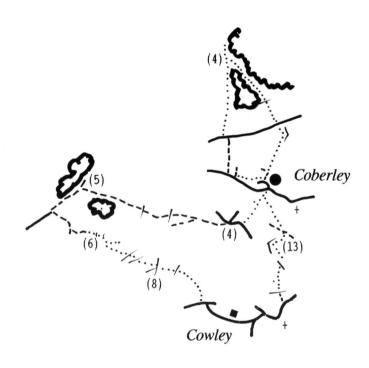

THE STROLL
About 2 miles on field paths and tracks, and skirting some nice woodland.

✳

(1) From car park take track "Seven Springs". Pass track L & power pole by stile, then up to A436.

(2) Go L 25yds & take steps opposite. Go with fence on your R & take field corner stile.

(3) Go ahead between woods to field end & take 1st stile L.

(4) Turn sharp L & go with wood on your L, over crest & down to A436.

(5) Take track opposite & go through farm to lane.

(6) Go L to pass end of farm drive & take small gate L. Go ahead parallel with R field edge & take hedge gap, then with wall on your R to village. ●

THE WALK
About 4.5 miles on tracks and grassy paths. There is a long stride over a great whaleback of a hill with fine views, then a plunge down a smooth and shapely dry valley, two of the most inviting features of the Cotswold contours.

✳

(1) From car park go down to Post Office & take kissing gate opposite.

(2) Follow path & take 2 stiles. Take stile AHEAD (not L), & keep same line by hedge to stile & track.

(3) Go ahead, pass barns on your R & follow track to lane bend. Go R 120 yds, pass lane R & take gate L to signposted track ◀

(4) Follow appx 1 mile (passing gate & track L, wood & farm L) to T junction on edge of wood.

[The area of young trees in plastic tubes is an embryonic wood on land given to the Woodland Trust. Round the outside is quick growing but shrubby hazel and birch ▶

(73)

which will nurse the enclosed ash and beech. (You can play "guess the sapling".) Both these big trees should do well on this well drained alkaline land, but beech needs early protection. The high fence is to exclude elephants.]

(5) Go L 500yds to kennels sign. Take drive L thro kennels, past R fork to house, & on grass track to gate. DON'T TAKE IT.

(6) Take path L past house to open field. Bear R & DOWN steep valley to ash tree & fenced area.

(7) Take gate, then stile, & go with hedge on your L to valley bottom. Go up to top L field corner (past L end of tree row) to hunting stiles.

(8) Take L stile & go with wall then fence on your L, & take hedge gap under big ash.

(9) Bear R & go with hedge on your R down to lane junction.

(10) Take lane opposite appx .6 mile thro village (Cowley), passing lane R & lane L, then Cowley Manor, to next R bend & Churnside Camp sign.

(11) Take camp track then stile, & on ahead to take mid fence stile. Go ahead to pass midfield tree clump on your L, & take midhedge stile by gate.

(12) Go L down field edge & via stile to field corner. Go R with hedge to field corner & cross bridge.

(13) Go ahead, pass projecting fence corner on your R & take field corner stile to track.

(14) Take stile opposite, cross field diagonally & take stile. Keep same line to village & via stiles to start. ●

(74)

River Churn at Coberley

Tributary of the Windrush near Guiting Power

(75)

Guiting Power

WHERE
Map reference SP 095248, a village off the B4068, about six
miles west of Stow on the Wold.

PARK & START
Park at the Village Hall and make sure that you put more in
the box than they ask. The Stroll and Walk start from the
green.

THE VILLAGE
Guiting is Old English for an outpouring of water, and
Guiting Power (from Le Poer, a local family) is to the south
of the village of Temple Guiting. It stands on the upper
reaches of the River Windrush, which the Walk crosses at two
fords in the hamlet of Kineton

Guiting Power is a small group of cream and grey stone houses
of different heights and sizes round a nicely kept green. The
medieval looking cross is post World War I. There is a school
(threatened), two pubs, a shop, a bakery and a village hall.
This is extraordinary for a small village when some people
may have to go miles for newspapers. Part of the reason

is that in the 1970's Mr Raymond Cochrane, who owned half of the village houses, gave them to a Trust on the terms that they were to be let to local people at modest rents.

Mr Cochrane also gave seventeen acres around some old fish ponds to the Gloucestershire Wildlife Trust. It is now managed as a reserve with habitat ranging from water, through marsh, to valleyside.

St Michael's church was originally Norman and some ancient features were retained in the restoration of 1903. Go and look at the door with its very typical Norman carving, which features amongst other things, an hour glass, finely carved column heads and a chequer pattern. (It is usually closed, says a glum little notice, because of repeated thefts.) Excavation in a field nearby has revealed the foundations of a tiny Saxon church and other long vanished buildings.

The wooded valley of the stream which you walk near the start is rich in limestone flowers, with scabious, meadow cranesbill and St John's Wort. In summer, butterflies and birds enrich the little wood and the upstream banks are ideal habitat for ferns, liverworts and horsetails.

THE STROLL
Some 2.25 miles on paths and tracks and a few lanes, but out here even these have grass down the middle. There is an lovely (muddy) wooded dingle and a couple of fords.

✳

(1) From village green go up past Post Office & take 1st lane R to its end.

(2) Take gate ahead & follow path down to fork by stream.

(3) Go R over tiny bridge & up via small gate, then with fence on your R to lane. [The medieval village was in the field right.] Walk takes gate ahead ►

(77)

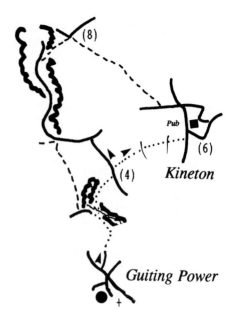

(4) Stroll goes L on drive to junction, then down L to cross ford. Go 75yds up to junction.

(5) Go L & via gate, & appx .3 mile to lane & farm.

(6) Go L down to dingle & meet path. Go R to join lane, & L to start. ●

Pub

(6)

(4)   *Kineton*

Guiting Power

THE WALK
About 4.5 miles of tracks and paths and tiny lanes.
The Cotswolds play their engaging trick on this route of resembling the most remote uplands, and at times you could be in Radnorshire or Yorkshire. You meet a witchy sort of dingle, the remains of a medieval village (nothing), a tree house, and a rock carved into a huge and amiable toad.

✳

Paras (1) to (3) as Stroll

(4) At lane, take gate ahead to pass house on your R & take 2 stiles. Go with hedge on your R to crest. [See the little dry pond with ash and sycamore trees.]

(5) Take stile & jink L, then with hedge on your R down to lane. Go L 25 yds, then R down to cross ford.

(6) Go L to bend & take track L to houses L. Track goes on, you cross ford to pass houses on your R, & up to junction.

(78)

(7) Go R a few paces & take lane (Roel Gate) 250yds, to take track R. Follow appx .5 mile to junction of road bend & tracks.

(8) Take grass track L past toad stone, & down to cross mill race to track.

[We would welcome any information on this cheerful creature. See the coppiced hazel on your right and later the silted mill pond. Spot the leaves in the wood that follows, there are poplar, sycamore, willow, hazel, oak, ash and some hornbeam.]

(9) Go L, & via gate by cottage to cross roads. Go ahead via gate & appx .3 mile to lane & farm.

(10) Go L down to dingle & meet path. Go R to join lane & L to start.

".... my mother made wonderful marmalade .... "

(79)

Ilmington

Map reference SP 210435. A village between the B4632
(formerly A46) and A429, about five miles north-east of
Chipping Campden.

PARK & START
Ilmington has a small and a large village green. Park near
and start from the large sloping one with the war memorial.

THE VILLAGE
Ilmington is Warwickshire's most appealing Cotswold village,
sitting on a distinct and shapely hill in deep rolling wold
country. This is the last flip of the Cotswolds, though the
great Jurassic Ridge continues north-east through Edge Hill
and towards the Northampton Hills.

This is a spacious village spread around the big sloping
green. About half the houses are on the level, at the edge of
the valley of the River Stour and effectively part of the
fertile, arable vale of Evesham. This is the Warwickshire
part. The rest of the village is spread across the foot of
the mighty hill in an abrupt change to a pastoral Cotswold
landscape. The road up Foxcote Hill has ominously frequent
grit containers, but from the crest you can view the whole
village and misty miles across the vale of Evesham.

Lanes of ginger stone cottages are linked by tempting
footpaths. But there are also houses of red brick with clay
tile roofs, some slate roofs and some thatch. In fact
Ilmington is a very happy mixture which avoids looking
preserved. There are two cosy inns, a hurdle maker's
workshop, an orchard and some ornamental lakes in the
middle of the village. Traces still exist of a horse drawn
tramway to Stratford.

Dreaming on the Green

(81)

On the lower side of the green is a fountain with a memorial plaque, to "those whose exertions" provided the village with a supply of pure water. In fact the springs were at one time thought to be so beneficial to health that the village might have grown into a prosperous spa, but Cheltenham and Leamington cornered the market.

Ilmington was famous for miles around for its mummers' plays and morris dancers led by Sam Bennett, "Last of the Troubadours", playing his 17th century fiddle. They were especially noted for their linked handkerchief dance "Maid of the Mill". Morris dancing is still a regular summer event.

The church of St Mary the Virgin is rich in monuments. In the rank of pollarded limes by the path are lamps in memory of Winifred Holman and Patty Bennett which fit very well with the rows of worn and slightly tumbled gravestones and tombs. But squatting next to the front door is what looks like a bad tempered wedding cake ringed with mean iron railings. Poor James Sansom.

The church has a Norman doorway and tower with a sundial on the south wall. Inside are urbane wrought iron wall lamp brackets with the subtle curves of superior craftsmanship. These sophisticated fittings enhance the simple, massive Norman arches at east and west ends. Plain bright window glass emphasises the glowing east window. The square and restrained oak pews have the merest trace of carving, and the craftsman left eleven little signatures in the form of mice. The modern organ is splendidly cased in light oak, built by a craftsman from nearby Mickleton.

The elegant manor house passed on the walk is Foxcote House, seat of the Howard family who gave their name to one of the pubs.

THE STROLL
About 1.5 miles on grassy fieldpaths, including a path through the village and a sample excursion into a glorious landscape.

*

(1) Face fountain on lower edge of green. Go L a few yards to Apple Tree Cottage & take path L

(2) Follow to church, go R to R bend & take kissing gate ahead.

(3) Go ahead with lake on your R & straight past fence corner to kissing gate & road. Go R & take kissing gate R of school.

(4) Follow fenced path & round L bend to take stile. Go ahead & take stile. Keep same line & take stile appx 30 yds R of field corner. ◀

(5) Go L & round field edge, via stile, to top of slope & take stile L.

(6) Go half L across hollow & take stile under power pole. Cross field diagonally, via midfence stile, & take stile.

(7) Go with hedge on your L to field corner & take stile. Cross field to 20yds L of cottage, take stile & down steps to lane

(8) Go R appx 18 paces & take path L. Cross stream & up to fence corner to take stile L. Cross field, take kissing gate, & follow lane back to start.

●

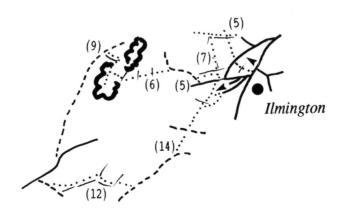

Ilmington

(83)

THE WALK
About 5 miles with some exhilarating (ie steep) contours.
There are magnificent views north over the Vale of Evesham,
lone barns on the hills, mysterious masts and a fairly
stately home.

✳

(1) At war memorial face church, then go L & take LOWER of 2 No Through Roads to pass Barn House.

(2) Follow to end of metalled surface & take path ahead (not R), then small gate.

(3) Go ahead & take stile. Go R & via path to lane. Go R a few paces & take steps.

(4) Cross stile, then field, up to next stile. DON'T TAKE IT. Go L along hedge to field end & bend R to join track.

(5) Follow appx 500yds to R bend & farm. Go ahead via 2 gates, & with hedge on your L go down to take gate.

(6) Go ahead to cross shoulder of hill appx 50 yds L of tree on crest, & down to take small gate.

◀

(7) Go R, take next small gate & cross stream. Go up with hedge on your R & take small gate L of field corner. Climb thro young trees to green track.

(8) Go R to open field. Go L up field edge to lane.

(9) Go L appx .7 mile to masts R & meet road.

[These technological totem poles were put up by the BBC to ward off evil spirits and commercial radio.]

(10) Take road ahead appx 500yds, to Ebrington Hill sign & take track L.

(11) Follow appx 200yds & take small gate L. Go ahead to meet projecting corner of R hedge, then follow field edge path via gate to field corner.

▶

(84)

(12) Go R, take small gate, then down field edge & take bottom corner stile. Bear L & take gate at R end of farm, to track.

(13) Go L past farm & follow drive, via bends, to fork by cattle grid R. Go L, cross next grid, & on appx 200yds to take yellow arrowed path L.

(14) Go up to crest, cross track & down field edge to face stile ahead. DON'T CROSS.

(15) Go R via 2 stiles to green track. Go L to lane, then L to start.

Minchinhampton

WHERE
Map reference SO 872008, a village off the A419, four miles
east of Stroud. Look for the signposts from the main road.

PARK & START
Bell Lane by the church.

THE VILLAGE
Minchinhampton is now more a big village than a cloth making
town, but there is much evidence of its prosperous past. Go
and see the ample Market House built in 1698. It stands on
tapered stone columns with an internal line of timber
supports, and on one of the walls is the Scale of Charges.

Minchinghampton Fayre is held every two years. Stalls are
erected in streets closed to traffic and the people go about
in costume to collect for charity.

Cheese and fresh fish stalls in the market

The town's name means "Hampton of the nuns", since the Manor was presented by William I's wife Matilda to a convent at Caen in Normandy. This explains why the 600 acre Common supported 1700 of the Convent's sheep. It includes "the Bulwarks", a series of mounds and ditches thought to have been Iron Age defences. Now people ride horses on the Common, play golf, fly kites and model aircraft, study limestone loving plants, make love and loll about in the sun. It is the second largest Common in Gloucestershire and belongs to the National Trust; nearby are several smaller ones, all worth exploring.

Tom Long's Post stands on the Common, a six fingered signpost at the central crossroads which was named after a highwayman who was hanged there.

Holy Trinity church was originally Norman but the oldest parts now standing are 14th century. The south transept of 1308 is lovely, with an unusual roof made entirely from stone. The spire is oddly truncated but attractive. The original standard model proved too heavy for the tower and the operation was performed in 1563. The interior walls and the ceiling of the nave are finished with bland perfection in smooth white plaster. This was the outcome of "restoration" carried out (executed) in 1842, when the old nave and chancel with their Norman arches were totally demolished and rebuilt. Neither is there anything half hearted about the rich and complicated stained glass, but there are several distinct styles which are worth comparing.

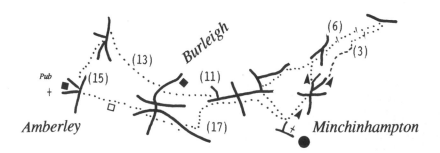

THE STROLL

A little under 1.5 miles over the Common, with some views over the wider landscape.

*

(1) From Bell Lane walk UP to Common. Go with wall on your R to corner. Bear R to crossroads.

(2) Take lane "Unsuitable for Wide Vehicles" appx 120yds, & cross steel stile L.

(3) Head for L field corner, stile & drive. Take stile opposite, &

with fence on your L down to signpost & path.

(4) Go L via stiles to lane.

(5) Go L appx 50yds & take stone stile L. Head for top R field corner, then via path & super squeeze stile to lane.

(6) Go up L to road. Bear L over Common back to church.

THE WALK

About 5 miles round Minchinhampton Common and a little of the nearby countryside. This walk takes in another much smaller Common - Besbury, a narrow strip of land on a ledge high on the south flank of the Golden Valley. It is less spectacular than Minchinhampton, but there are leafy views over the huge landscape structures of hills and valleys.

*

(1) From Bell Lane walk UP to Common. Go with wall on your R to corner. Bear R to crossroads.

(2) Cross & take lane "Unsuitable for Wide Vehicles" a few paces. Take lane R appx 700 yds (passing street R, lane becomes track) to end. Take stone stile.

(3) Go R with wall on your R appx 400yds to stone trough. Go down L past power pole to signpost, & take stile.

(4) Go L down to lane. Go L 30 yds & take steel stile L, then next stile.

(5) Go ahead over side of hump, then with wood edge on your L thro hedge gap.

(6) Bear L to pass power pole on your R & take stile in wall. Pass house on your L to lane

(7) Go up L & round R bend to fork. Go up L appx 50yds & take stile R.

(8) Follow path (past signpost) 600yds to lane.

(9) Go L appx 50yds & take stone stile L. Head for top R field corner, then via path & super squeeze stile to lane.

(10) Go L to road. Cross & go R, parallel with it. Cross Dr Brown's Rd & on to end of houses R.

(11) Cross road to corner of Common. Go diagonally between roads to far end of distant houses. Pass them & meet road.

(12) Cross at Burleigh sign. Follow field track passing upper of 2 midfield bushes on your R, to crosstrack with cottage down R.

(13) Go ahead 100yds & curve R with track 100yds. Look L & head for 2 fingered signpost on road.

(14) Cross road & go L with wall on your R. Wall bends R, you keep parallel with road. Pass 1st house L & bear L to war memorial

(15) Cross road. See shrubby hawthorns ahead, pass them on your R & follow low bank. Head for L of reservoir fence.

(16) Go on to tall chimneyed house in trees, then pass, to front wall of RED chimneyed house.

[You will have realised that this Common is something rare and special. Why then, the network of busy roads, traffic fumes and constant noise?]

(17) Go with wall on your R via bends & cross Dr Brown's Road [Note stately gates looking for a home.] back to start. ●

(89)

North Nibley

WHERE
Map reference SP 740958, a village on the B4060 about one and
a half miles south-west of Dursley.

PARK & START
The village straddles the B4060 with its centre at the cross
roads by the Black Horse pub. The main street to the west is
Barrs Lane where parking is very limited. Find space in The
Street, on the east side. Start from the Black Horse, from
inside if you wish.

THE VILLAGE
North Nibley has twice made a mark on English history.
Dominating the village is the 111 foot high tower built in
1866 to commemorate William Tyndale. He was born at Nibley
in 1484 and burnt at the stake in 1536 for translating the
Bible into English.

No doubt, if you like towers the Tyndale Memorial is one for
your collection. Square and tapered in grey Cotswold stone,
the upper half is Italianate and romantic with tiny arrow-
slot windows, which might accommodate darts. Beneath the
campanile roof are dark round-headed windows, from which a
young lady named Brunhilde (or something), will let down
golden tresses to collect the milk and newspapers. The
lower half of the tower is sombrely, gothically, Victorian.
Under seriously pointed arches, blank stone panels invite
your conscience to suggest what will be written there on
Judgement Day. Do these arches reflect two working rules
of Victorian ecclesiastical architecture; (1) Gothic points
induce sanctity, and (2) a building's spiritual worth is
inversely proportionate to the angle? The base of the tower
is defended by iron graveyard railings.

From the knoll on which the tower stands there are wide views over the Severn Valley (Vale of Berkeley) to the Forest of Dean and beyond. From the top they are even better, if you care to borrow a key from The Stores in Barrs Lane, or Knoyle House on the main road opposite the approach track.

St Martin's church is light and lofty. It probably has Saxon origins but the earliest work to be seen is 15th century, notably the roof of the nave. Note the fretted infilling of the truss structure. The chancel is a Victorian repro job. We might regret the loss of what it replaced, but like most work of the period, it was well and reverently done. There is a fine gold mosaic reredos and ochre wall decorations in recollection of medieval styles. The wooden (not brass) eagle on the lectern seems to be waiting for a tit-bit, and all through the sermons the quiet thud-thud of the clock lulls the congregation to sleep. The south aisle was added by the Earl of Berkeley in 1470 in thanks for his victory in a takeover bid, see below. Nearby stand a quaint Chantry House and an early Victorian village school.

The village's second mark on history was made in 1470, when at Nibley Green to the north-west was fought the last private (military) battle between rival barons to take place in England. The Talbots unsuccessfully challenged the Berkeleys for their estates and 150 men were killed. These days it is done by buying shares and boardroom coups.

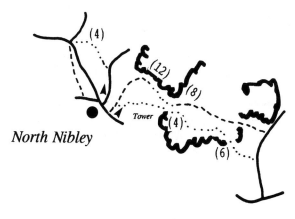

North Nibley

(91)

The Tyndale Memorial

THE STROLL
This 1.5 miles Stroll is as high on interest and variety as
the Walk. A rolling green pastoral landscape appears quite
suddenly, there is a hasty little stream with a soggy bed
full of water plants, and an ancient hedged track.

As you climb the track, look at the doorway to nowhere. The
carved capital stone is certainly attractive, but what is the
meaning of the inscription - NMMH SPNC AD 1607?

*

(1) From Black Horse take Barrs Lane, pass street R & take L fork.

(2) Follow appx 100yds to R bend. Cross cattle grid into gateway & go appx 30yds to take path R.

(3) Pass cottage on your R & take stile to field. Go with hedge on your L, via stile, & down to take stile L into wood.

(4) Cross bridge. [But stop to look at the wild celandines, kingcups and celery, and in the drier ◀ spots, bluebells and wild garlic (or ransoms).] Follow path R to lane.

(5) Go L to B4060. CARE. Take track opposite (past doorway R) & up to lane.

[Grandly classical & flagpoled Nibley House, right, is a sort of compact-model stately. Outside a lopsided sign offers potatoes in 25kg bags.]

(6) Go L to start. ●

St Martin's

(93)

The end of the Walk

(94)

THE WALK

About 4 miles, mainly through Westridge Wood which is rich in wild flowers, creatures and birds. You visit the Tyndale Monument from which there are terrific views over the Severn Estuary, and similar views are sustained for about a mile. You also pass over Brackenbury Ditches, a six acre triangular Iron Age hill fort, now rather lost in woodland. Towards the end is a quarry and a deep holloway, the purpose of which we leave you to work out. There is one steep climb and descent.

✳

(1) From Black Horse, take B4060 towards Wotton etc appx 100yds, & take track L up to steps R.

(2) Follow steps up to Monument.

[The Vale of Berkeley lies below, mild and green. To the north-west is the Severn Estuary with bridge.

(3) Go with fence on your R past topograph & curve R to enter wood. Take (bust?) gate & go on 20yds to track junction.

(4) Keep R & follow wide track across hillside. ◀

[Above are larch with a few Scots pine and a shrub layer of hazel and birch. But below the conifers have been replaced with beech and ash, native trees which should do well on the alkaline soil. The view of the Severn and the Vale is sustained along this shelf.]

◀ *Track dips then rises, passes track from R, then levels at clearing with tracks L & R.*

(5) Go R, pass track R, to T junction. Go R on wood edge track to 2 white posts at wood corner.

(6) Go ahead in banked track to lane (Old London Road). Go L appx .5 mile & take 1st earth track L (Bridleway sign).

(7) Follow appx 250yds & take gate at wood corner, then with wood on your R, pass 2 tracks R to 5 ways junction at wood corner.
▶

(95)

[In the next section you can play spot the conifer, Scots pine, western red cedar and Norway spruce.]

(8) Take track ahead (ie 3rd from L); at fork go L to wood edge & crosstracks.

(9) Go ahead, pass 2 forks R & small path L, then on 12 paces & take path R.

(10) Follow to cross track & on to former (bust?) gate. Go to wood edge.

(11) Bear R from outward route, parallel with wood edge R, & take gate into wood.

[Go and see the old stone quarry on the left. Now softened and recovered by nature, the amphitheatre calls out for drama and music, probably involving the young lady from the tower.]

(12) Follow track down via gate & deep holloway to road. Go R to start. ●

Tomb of John Bryan, Mason, at Painswick

Painswick

WHERE
Map reference SO 866096. The village is on the A46 about three miles north of Stroud.

PARK & START
Stamages Lane car park by the A46, south of the church.

THE VILLAGE
This elegant grey stone village is often called "Queen of the Cotswolds". It stands on high ground over the Painswick Valley where the Painswick Stream, which once powered the town's mills, runs down to the River Frome.

Narrow streets of merchants' houses were built in the boom years of the wool trade, though Painswick's wealth came from cloth rather than yarn, and many date from the 17th and 18th centuries. The stone quarried from Painswick Beacon is cream coloured when new but weathers to silver grey. Streets near the church were badly damaged by World War II bombing but have been lovingly restored. Look out for the fine half timbered post office, and in spring visit the Rococo Gardens of Painswick House to admire the drifts of snowdrops.

The front doors of Painswick houses usually open onto the street, giving the town a close and intimate atmosphere. There are few front gardens so the large central churchyard is an important open space. Here rows of plumply sculpted yew trees are clipped so hard that the lichened gravestones seem more alive. There are supposed to be ninety nine, and efforts to grow one hundred yews have been frustrated by the Devil because he always causes one tree to wither and die. We find it alarming that he is not under better control in Painswick, and if you count the trees you will find that their sums are not too good either.

The lychgate is made of old timbers from the belfry; there are bells carved on two bargeboards and roses on another. The churchyard is said to have the best collection of Georgian tombs anywhere, but perhaps not many people collect them. Chest, pedestal and tea caddy tombs and anything else you fancy to lie in, they are mostly the work of the local Bryan family of master masons. The oddest is a stark stone pyramid, tomb of John Bryan who died in March 1774.

St Mary's church was built in the 12th century and rebuilt in the 14th. Walk around it and study the slender spire. Now ... is is wonky or not? The east window is ornate but its Victorian spirit is with its medieval surroundings. At the west end is a classical screen of black marble columns and ornamental white plaster with a formidable mahogany door. Where do you think it would look best? More warm hearted are the hand embroidered woollen kneelers made by members of the Mothers' Union between 1964 and 1984. Designs include crosses, flowers, views, christenings, silver weddings, crests, the Great Western Railway and goodness knows what. But they all match because of the Vicar's decision that they should have the same blue background.

Go and see the one twentyfifth scale model of the three masted *Bonaventure,* Drake's flagship before the Armada. The original was built in 1580 and the model in 1885.

THE STROLL
A 2 mile wander which starts on field paths but becomes a circular tour of the outskirts of the town. Returning to the centre you walk stone streets of magnificent little houses and humbler but beautiful cottages; most people would be happy in either. Look for Dover House and Loveday's House built about 1720, which are said to be the best of Cotswold early Georgian. The same local stone and the local traditions of the masons imposed a carefree and unconscious harmony on a great variety of tastes and preferences. Could anything like it be done now? The discipline of local materials and styles has had to be replaced by Planning Law which has played a large part in preserving what you can see.

(1) From car park go uphill to lychgate R. Take lane OPPOSITE 250yds to gate L & Cotswold Way.

(2) Go L down field edge & take stile. Follow path to track.

(3) Take stile L & follow path thro gardens to stile & field. Go down with fence on your R & take stile.

(4) Follow L fence 70 yds & take stile L. Go ahead & take stile in projecting fence corner to track. Go on to bend, then ahead via gateway to A46. ◢

(5) Take lane opposite appx .7 mile (over cross roads) to T junction.

(6) Go down R appx 50 yds & take 1st drive L a few paces. Take path L by railings appx 250 yds up to street.

(7) Go L, pass lane R & take next L, then ahead into churchyard. Pass church on your L to lychgate. Go L to start. ●

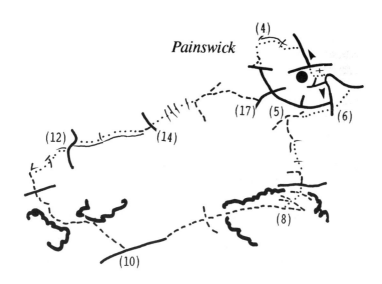

Painswick

(99)

THE WALK

About 5 miles of tracks through fields and woodland with some quiet lanes. About half the walk lies in the Painswick Valley and half on the hilltops.

(1) From car park go uphill to lychgate R & into churchyard. Pass church on your L & exit R via tree arch.

[See the iron framed "spectacle" stocks outside the churchyard.]

(2) Take Hale Lane ahead to bottom. Go L to T junction, then down R.

(3) Follow [past well left] 400yds (past lane R) to cross bridge.

(4) Take narrow lane R appx 250yds to house. Pass its front & take path. Pass track R & round L bend to fork of tracks.

(5) Go L up track to stile & field. Go with hedge on your R via 2 stiles to track. Go ahead to lane.

(6) Take path opposite & cross stile. Go up field edge to corner & take path R, via stile, to track.

(7) Take path opposite up to track junction. Go R a few paces & turn sharp L up rising track 15 paces. Take path R up to track.

(8) Go R & follow wood edge track appx .4 mile to end, & take stile. Keep same line to stile & track junction.

(9) Take track opposite & pass farm, then on lane appx 400yds, to gates either side & track R.

[Behind left are views of a hill, whorled and scarped by quarrying but now greened over. Ahead is the village of Pitchcombe. Soon you will see Stroud, crowded by big headlands and shoulders of hills.]

(10) Take track R over crest, to enter wood & meet track. Go down L .5 mile (past track L) to road.

(100)

(11) Take track opposite to green silos & take stile R. Go with barns on your L & follow field edge to take corner stile. Go parallel with L hedge, take corner stile & cross track to lane.

(12) Go L appx 100yds & take gate R. Take stile ahead, then with ha-ha wall on your R, go on to take 2 stiles.

(13) Go with hedge on your R 500yds [This field has more springs than a double bed] ; head 50 yds L of field corner & take gate. Follow track to lane.

(14) Take stile opposite & go ahead, pass power pole on your L & take stile. Bear R with field edge & cross bridge.

(15) Bear up L & take field corner stile. Go ahead to L side of house & kissing gate to track.

(16) Go ahead on drive & lane appx .4 mile (past track L) to meet lane.

(17) Go L, cross bridge, go up over cross roads & appx 150yds to pass house Howbeg R. Take green track R to lane.

(18) Go up L to Fig Tree Cottage R. Take path opposite (Hale Lane) to church. Go L to lychgate then L to car park. ●

The Front Row

(101)

South Cerney

WHERE
Map reference SU 050973, a village off the A419 about four
miles south-east of Cirencester.

PARK & START
Church Lane or Silver Street just north of the river bridge.

SOUTH CERNEY & DISTRICT

The village takes its name from the River Churn, which flows
from south of Cheltenham, through South Cerney and on for
three miles to the Thames at Cricklade. Or does it become the
Thames? The Churn is claimed as the source because it is the
most remote headwater from the mouth. [See our entry on
Coberley, where this is touched on again.] At Cricklade the
Churn is joined by the River Ray, the Swill Brook and some
nameless trickles.

The whole area is very flat and watery. Apart from the river
and numerous streams, the village is surrounded by flooded
gravel pits which have been landscaped into lakes to form
the Cotswold Water Park. An information board passed on the
Walk explains that the ground is really a great gravel basin
through which water is continually moving from north-west to
south-east. In fact much of the gravel was extracted from
underwater by draglines, avoiding Canute-like attempts to
keep the workings dry.

Until the 1960's South Cerney also had a railway. The line
from Gloucester to Swindon was built in 1883 by the Midland &
South Western Junction Railway Co, which remained independent
until it became part of the GWR in the 1923 grouping. You can
see some of the structures on the Stroll and Walk.

South Cerney has some quaintly named streets. Look out for
Upper Up, Clakes Hay and Bow Wow. The main road is Silver

Street. Church Lane is plain enough, but leads to the magnificent 12th century All Hallows church.

In grey stone with magnificently carved doorways and a fine chancel, this is a large and lofty church with an oddly squat tower on which is a painted sundial. The parishioners obviously liked Victorian stained glass and decided to have as much as possible. In the churchyard is an unusually beautiful chest tomb of 1370. It bears the carved figures of the occupants, man and wife, with their hands crossed over their chests.

Near the river is a handsome 18th century octagonal gazebo, and by the canal on the Walk at Cerney Wick, another circular building. The Roundhouse is a sort of stumpy, unilluminated lighthouse built to house the lock keeper, and is still someone's home.

The Thames & Severn Canal was built in 1779 to link the River Thames from its highest navigable point at Lechlade, to Stroud. The Stroudwater Canal led down to the River Severn. The 2.25 miles long Sapperton Tunnel took the T&S under the watershed. It was abandoned in 1933 and you can see the dereliction as you walk. But the Cotswold Canals Trust is pursuing an ambitious long term scheme to restore full navigation, and some locks and pounds have already been rescued.

THE STROLL
About 1.5 miles on footpaths and a quiet lane, visiting the church, and the derelict Thames & Severn Canal.

Follow Walk paras
(1) - (3), then;

(4) Go R appx 500yds to lane. Go R back to start.

●

[Take the steps down by the old railway bridge to see the unusual structure. This is one of several local bridges in a style used by the Midlands & South Western Junction Railway.]

The Roundhouse, Cerney Wick

(104)

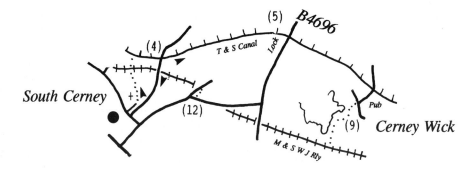

THE WALK

About 5.5 miles with some fieldpaths, but this is essentially a trip out on the old canal towpath and back on the old railway. In such a wet, low lying area of old gravel pits and lakes in flat fields, there is not a hill to be found. But this easy style of walking brings its own pleasures- the trees, the water plants and the wildlife of the canal, and the strange red brick viaducts of the railway. There are loos on the way, and an information board explaining the geology and hydrology of the area.

✱

(1) From junction of Church Lane & Silver Street, go to church. Take path on R of church gate to kissing gate.

(2) Fork L & curve L to take stile. Bear R to cross drive & take midwall stone stile. Keep same line & cross stone stile in hedge.

(3) Bear L & under railway to take stile. Go ahead to field corner & take stile to canal towpath. ◀

◀*(4) Go R appx .6 mile (crossing lane) to lock & brick arch. DON'T CROSS.*

(5) Take 2 stiles R, & with hedge on your L to B4696. Cross & take stile to footbridge. ▶

[Loos on R. Loos apart, this is a fine easy walk between two naturally grown lines of trees. The dewatered canal is a better habitat for wildlife than boats, but here and there you can see signs of restoration work. The most obviously important structures are

(105)

the locks, but all the culverts and overflow systems have to work. You can see that the bed of the canal still holds water which is a testimony to the endurance of puddled clay. The banks may need reinforcement in places and this can be prolonged and expensive work.]

(6) From footbridge fork L. Follow towpath appx .4 mile & pass roundhouse L to road.

(7) Go R & pass Crown pub to T junction.

(8) Take stile ahead & follow field edge to stile & lane. Take stile opposite, then 2 stiles to lake.

(9) Go ahead beside lake. Curve R with it, then curve L, to lake corner & mark post L.

(10) Take steps & bridge then follow field edge to stile & old railway.

(11) Go R appx .3 mile to B4696.

[The curious viaduct of red English bonded bricks with oval pierced piers is one of several on this walk. This construction was adopted by the Midlands and South Western Junction Railway for road bridges. On top is a timber platform from which you can scan the landscape for birds or Russian spies.]

(10) Continue on railway to road.

[The gawky, pastel tinted timber chalets by the lake on your right are "lakeside lodges". With three bedrooms and two bathrooms, the sign says they are very exclusive, perhaps because few people need so many bathrooms.]

(11) Go L to end of trees R. Pass double gate R & take small gate to path.

(12) Follow under bridge & along old railway appx 250yds to next bridge.

(13) Take steps L up to lane. Go R back to start.

(106)

Road over rail bridge, M&SWJ Railway

Stanton

WHERE
Map reference SP 068343, a village off the B4632 (formerly A46) between Broadway & Winchcombe.

PARK & START
Village car park (free).

THE VILLAGE
This little honey and grey village climbs the Cotswold edge towards the wooded summit of Shenberrow Hill. It is is often mentioned as one of the loveliest in the Cotswolds. The single main street of cottages, houses and farms has many 17th century datestones and the buildings all bear a curious likeless, beyond the usual Cotswold features. Notice too the scattering of timber framed houses in the lower section of the street.

Stanton was badly in need of a face lift in 1906 when a wealthy Lancashire mill designer, Sir Philip Stott, bought the estate. He restored the neglected houses, piped in a water supply and built a swimming pool. The timber framed houses were brought from local villages to fill in gaps and were rebuilt exactly as they had been in their prime. So the harmonious character of the village may be due to this single grand refurbishment carried out early in the century.

Sir Philip Stott did more, he brought in the leading church architect Sir Ninian Comper to refurbish and beautify St Michael and all Angels. A Saxon church once stood on the site, but the earliest work in the present building is Norman, with later additions and extensions common to most Cotswold churches in the 13th and 15th centuries. There are two pulpits, the original was used from 1375 for 300 years, but replaced by the present upstart which was once used by Charles Wesley for an early sermon. Apart from restoring the building, Sir Ninian designed the rood screen, reredos and east windows. The brass candle holders are modern.

THE STROLL
Nearly 3 miles on grassy field paths at the foot of the slope between the Cotswold Hills and the Vale of Evesham. There are views over the hedges and fields running level to the horizon. Mud.

(1) From car park go R. Bend L past lane R & follow main street. Pass cross L & up to phone box & post box.

(2) Take drive L to bend & cross stile ahead. Go ahead & pass power pole on your L, then with fence on your R to take stile.

[Watch for a stumpy ash on your left with many branches, which seems to have been pollarded. This was similar to coppicing to produce poles, but the shoots were out of reach of grazing animals.]

(3) Go ahead with hedge on your L, keep same line on clear field path & take stile or kissing gate.

(109)

(4) Bear R to pass FAR end of wood, take hedge gap stile & cross stream. Go ahead to field end & take small gate.

(5) Keep same line, bear R past end of hedge & take stile. Go thro small wood to stream & meet path.

[Long ago the big old willows were pollarded, now they are grown over with wild roses. In autumn there are crimson hips against the orange and yellow leaves.]

(6) Go down L & take gate. Follow lane to tiny green at junction. ◄

(7) Go L, round S bends, pass drive L & round R bend, to last house L.

(8) Take stile L & go with fence then hedge on your L. Keep same line appx .5 mile along hedges & via stiles, to cross stile with gate R.

(9) Go parallel with hedge on your R appx 150 yds, & take bridge & iron gate R.

(10) Follow path to wall & go R. Pass church tower on your L & go round L, to gate & lane. Go R to road, & R to start. ●

Stanway's Golden Gateway

(110)

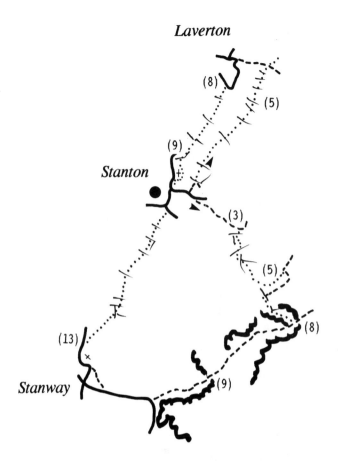

Laverton

(8)

(5)

(9)

Stanton

(3)

(5)

(8)

(13)

Stanway

(9)

THE WALK

About 5 miles with a steep climb up Shenberrow Hill giving
sweeping views. Near the hilltop farm are the remains of a
four acre Iron Age settlement which has yielded a bronze
bracelet, an iron knife and bone needles. Coming down again
through a fine belt of woodland you meet a hydraulic ram.

In the village of Stanway you pass the amazing gatehouse to
Stanway House (see below), a huge and magnificent tithe barn
of 1370 and a thatched cricket pavilion given to the village
by Sir James Barrie, author of Peter Pan.

(111)

✳

(1) From car park go R. Bend L past lane R & follow main street appx 300yds to fork.

(2) Go R [NB Follow Cotswold Way sign, yellow arrow & white disc] . Take gate & on appx 300yds NEARLY to conifers by reservoir.

(3) Take path down R & cross stile, then on to next. Go with hedge on your R, then clear rising path & take field top stile.

(4) Go with hedge on your L & take stile, then clear rising path joins level path. Go up R via small valley to crest, & take gate L of farm.

(5) Go on appx 200yds to junction. Go R via cattle grid & follow track thro farm. Pass track L & take gate.

(6) Go with beeches on your R & take gate, then along wall & take stile. Bear L & take midwall stile. ◢

(7) TURN L on field edge, enter wood & take track to its end at track junction.

(8) Go R, pass track R & enter wood. Follow track over cross track & down appx .6 mile past tracks R & L to bottom.

[The mad blacksmith noise is a hydraulic ram. Water from above is piped into the base of a cylinder and pushes up a piston. When it rises a few inches the water escapes and the piston falls back, to be lifted again. The persistent short movement can be used to pump water and generate electricity.]

(9) Pass gate R, take track on wood edge. Keep to edge .5 mile down to lane.

(10) Go R to B4077 & follow .3 mile, past phone box R, to near road sign (Wood Stanway etc). ▶

[Note the little wooden pagoda thingy with interesting figurines.]

(112)

(11) Take stile R, curve R with ditch on R, then follow clear path to lane. Go R to T junction and R thro village.

[The golden gatehouse to Stanway House has been called a gallimaufry of architectural styles. Built at some point between 1620 and 1637 we have cosily mullioned Tudor windows, twee Dutch gables, baby classical pillars, a hammy broken pediment arch and bulky square fretted balconies, all embellished with roses and shells on stalks. But it is seriously grand and sees nothing funny in all this.

This is one of the most enjoyable buildings you could meet, but don't pass St Peter's, a small plain Norman church. There is a brightly woven altar cloth, and a brass lectern on which the eagle seems to be trying to peck at an itch.]

(12) Pass stone roofed tithe barn R & thatched tennis pavilion to ditto cricket pavilion(!).

(13) Take stile R and follow clear field path via stiles appx 1 mile, to stile & lane by red barn.

(14) Go L to road, then R to junction, & L to start.

●

(113)

Turkdean

WHERE
Map reference SP 107175, a hilltop village a mile and a half
north-west of the A40 - A429 junction, just north of
Northleach.

PARK & START
Park in the village near the church, from where the Walk and
Stroll both start.

THE VILLAGE
A quiet little hilltop village, unlike most others in the
Cotswolds which lie low in the valleys.

The exotic name has nothing to do with Turkey or Turks, there
is not even a pub called the Saracen's Head, in fact there is
no pub at all. The name (learned people say) probably came
from the Saxon word for a river valley, which given its
position seems pretty odd, or from the Norman surname la
Tourque.

Tiny All Saints church is thought to be be one of the oldest
in the Cotswolds. Norman architecture at the tower end was
followed by examples of work from most later periods, and
the walls of the tower contain a variety of carved stones
used in different restorations. The bells are very old and
may have been cast in the 1400's. The rood screen is painted
with butterflies and green tendrils on a cream background,
with edges picked out in black "barbers pole" stripes. You
may find All Saints charmingly decorated by parishoners with
leaves and flowers, depending on the time of year.

Turkdean has some grand old farms, and you may notice the
dove holes in some of the barn gables. The birds were a
valuable source of meat and eggs to supplement the monotonous
winter diet.

Turkdean's glory is its avenue of beech trees, beautiful in all seasons and offering habitat to tits, nuthatches and woodpeckers.

THE STROLL
About 1.5 miles with a leafy village path, a steep climb through the sheep and a track with fine views. Can be slippery after rain.

Follow Walk ✱

Paras (1) & (2) then:

`[As you climb the view widens to unveil tumbling hills, woods, hedges and walls.]`

`(3) Go R & up past buildings to road. Go R down to start.` ●

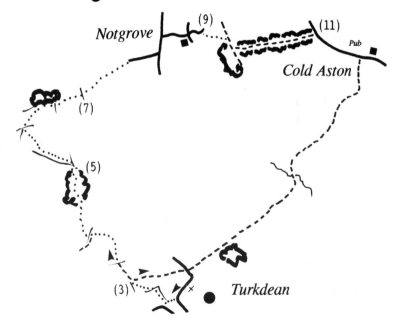

Notgrove (9) (11)

Pub

Cold Aston

(7)

(5)

(3) × *Turkdean*

THE WALK
Some 6 miles of grassy slopes and smooth glacial valleys.
There is a long avenue of beech trees and a rolling track
over the hills.

＊

*(1) From church go down
road, pass spring & trough
R & take path R. Go down
to level, cross stream &
take gate R.*

*(2) Go parallel with R
fence & take 1st gate R.
Climb diagonally to top L
field corner gate & track.*

*(3) Go L down track to
level & take R of 2 gates.*

*[A gorgeous curved valley,
sculpted long and smooth
by the glaciers.]*

*(4) Go with hedge on your
L & take next gate L.
Follow diagonal grass
track to far top corner
gate & barn.*

*(5) Pass barn. Go L with
wall on your L appx 330
yds to wooden markpost R.
Bear R, crossfield path
aims midway between 2
woods on horizon, to
corner.◀*

*(6) Turn half R & head for
near corner of wood. Go
down with wood on your L
to valley bottom.*

*[The wood has ash, beech,
limes, sycamore and horse
chestnuts but no visible
oak. Very much a wood of
limestone country.]*

*(7) Go up with fence on
your L & on to pass barn.
Follow lane to T junction.
Go L to junction & turn R.*

*[Here is a magical avenue
of beech and lime with a
dream of a cricket ground
on the right. On hazy
autumn afternoons, the
light and heavy rollers
sleep in the leaves and
the sight screens yawn
quietly by the pavilion.
A fallen sign prosaically
announces "Nats Sports
Cricket Club".]*

*(8) Follow lane across
junction & via S bends to
foot of slope by spreading
beech. ▶*

(9) Take gate R. Climb diagonally L to far top corner gate & track.

(10) Go R, then L into beech avenue, & follow to road.

[The autumn colours can be imagined. In the second part of the avenue, note the maple saplings, which have yellow autumn foliage. The close and random growth suggest self seeding, but the even age and overall pattern points to planning]

(11) Go R appx 500yds, passing houses L, & take lane R. Follow appx 2 miles to junction. Go L to start.

Limes and Beeches at Notgrove

Whittington

Map reference SP 014207, a village just off the A40 about
four miles east of Cheltenham.

PARK & START
By pavement near church, about 100yds off the A40. The Walk
and Stroll both start from here.

THE VILLAGE
Whittington is small and quiet in spite of the roaring A40,
and an ancient place. A Roman villa stood here and a medieval
village, now just a few humps in a field.

St Bartholomew's Church and Whittington Court are the most
outstanding buildings, and you see them at the start. The
tiny church is essentially Norman but has a wooden bellcote,
rare in the Cotswolds. It has practically disappeared beneath
an immense yew tree. Inside are striking reminders of past
inhabitants, with the tombs of two knights in 14th century
armour accompanied by a lady of the same period. There are
memorial brasses to members of the Cotton family who built
the Court, and outside a stone wall plaque in memory of Giles
Watkins, curate, who died in 1690. Rest in Peace, Mr Watkins,
like the chubby cherub on your plaque who seems to be asleep
with his mouth open.

Whittington Court is a beautiful Tudor building which quite
dwarfs the church and has been lovingly restored by its new
owners. It is sometimes open to the public, see the notice on
the gate.

The east end of the village has been decaying for some years
and restoration is now in hand. Notice the Victorian well
inscribed "Waste not want not", and note that you are invited
to subscribe to its repair. Datestones appear on some houses

and outside one is a weathered milestone. Get the children to hunt for the postbox, and date it, and to hunt for the former school. We are offering no prize in case they find them. Look too at the graceful stand of beeches which makes a perfect backdrop to the village.

THE STROLL
About 1.25 miles of level walking on field paths and lanes. You pass through the jolly flat medieval village, and the modern one.

(1) From Court gates, take kissing gate opposite. Go ahead to pass lone oak on your L & projecting field corner, to take field corner stile. Go with hedge on your L to corner, then L to gate & lane.

(2) Go L appx .5 mile, past road L, to junction with No Through Road.

(3) Go L & at end of cottage take (bust) kissing gate L. Go ahead, cross stream, then bear SLIGHTLY R over hill to meet L HEDGE, & take corner stile.

(4) Go with hedge on your R & pass gate R to take stile, then next stile to road.

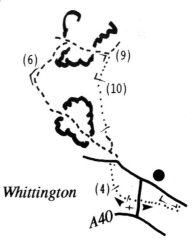

Whittington

THE WALK

About 3 miles on field paths, tracks and quiet lanes. There are two gorgeous woodland sections, a curiously natural looking abandoned quarry and one of those lonely tracks over the dome of a hill down to the valley. Hippos find it ecstatically muddy.

✳

(1) Face Court gates & take stile on R, & on to take next. Go parallel with L fence/hedge & take corner stile.

(2) Bear R & head for L end of long cottage, cross stream to (bust) kissing gate & lane.

(3) Go R to corner. Go L appx 300 yds, past lane R, to end of surface, & take gate ahead.

(4) Follow wood track .4 mile, via gate, & take wood end gate.

(5) Follow green track ahead, curving R with tree line on your L, then hedge, down to take gate.

(6) Go ahead between bushes, bearing R on field track. Pass path L & white mark post, to join L hedge & on to small gate into wood. ◢

(7) Follow wood edge path to junction. Take 2nd track R (past power pole) to wood edge gate & field.

(8) Go ahead with fence on your R, pass small gate R up to crest & gate R.

(9) Take stile R. Follow field edge track with hedge & wall on your R, to field end gateway. [see the sweeping down-like contours of the hills.]

(10) Cross field diagonally (if in doubt, sight row of poplars far ahead & head for middle) & take gate near corner.

(11) Follow track down to gate & lane. Go R to lane, then L to junction.

(12) Go ahead thro village & take lane R to start.

●